THE MONEY BUTTON

*Why Innovating at Big Companies is All About
You, Not Your Ideas*

Brian Pittenger

The Money Button

First Edition

ISBN 978-1-7320894-0-2

eISBN 978-1-7320894-1-9

2018-1

TABLE OF CONTENTS

to be facing as you start implementing innovative approaches)

EXCERPTS FROM AN INTERVIEW: "Mark"

CHAPTER FIVE: A shiv and potable drinking water for two – no, three! - days. (Or, Tools you'll need to survive)

EXCERPTS FROM AN INTERVIEW: "Rich"

CHAPTER SIX: Embracing your inner rampaging mother**er** (Or, how to get things done)

CHAPTER SEVEN: Black holes and other problems with your project (Or, What can go wrong, and other things that *definitely* will)

EXCERPTS FROM AN INTERVIEW: "Marta"

CHAPTER EIGHT: It could, *maybe*, be worth it, but probably not, but maybe! (Or, Career opportunities and risks associated with being this "maverick" you want to be so badly)

CHAPTER NINE: A significant waste of your valuable time (Or, some half-baked ideas your company could implement to nurture innovators, but ultimately won't)

CHAPTER TEN: I'd still recommend you didn't (Or, last words of advice)

<u>Super Inspirational Quote</u>

All major changes are like death – you can't see through to the other side until you are there.

- *Ian Malcolm (via Michael Crichton)[i]*

PROLOGUE, WHERE I PREEMPTIVELY DESTROY YOUR ILLUSIONS (BUT FEEL BAD ABOUT IT)

Let's just get this out there: I'm sorry.

I mean, this book can't help you be a successful innovator in a large company any more than it can keep your dog from sniffing crotches.   Destroying innovators is just instinctive for big companies!

What this book *can* do is share my experiences from a combined 20-plus year career working in giant organizations – mostly Fortune 500-sized.   This does not make me an expert in Organizational Change Management, or Organizational Theory, or even, uh, Organization?   In other words, I get it – I don't have a PhD in anything. I'm more of a 'practical' expert. In other words, *they* can tell you all about building a laser beam, how it works in theory, what its limits might be, etc. Instead, my book just goes about burning holes in stuff with an awesome laser gun and then has some thoughts about how I felt doing it and what happened next. My 'testing' and 'data' comes from what I've observed over-and-over again in year-after-year of being trapped in cubicles.

Also, and I can't tell you enough how much I regret this … you're going to notice in this book that I swear. I mean, shit, I swear what's going to seem like A Lot, especially for a professional business book (even though I'd strongly recommend the same to Stephen Covey if he'd ever take my fucking phone calls). And, much of this swearing could feel *personal* in nature, as if I caught you trying to budge in line in front of me at the DMV. But look at it from my side. I mean, *you're* seriously considering a role as an Innovator at a large company, so I figure you're either pretty resilient and will brush this off, or you're bat-shit crazy, in which case the voices in your head were probably already swearing at you.

Finally, if you ARE offended or put-off by this, by all means ...

PUT DOWN THIS BOOK IMMEDIATELY. SERIOUSLY, JUST DROP IT WHERE YOU STAND AND RUN! DON'T PUT IT BACK ON THE SHELF WHERE YOU FOUND IT – THAT'S WHAT THE BOOK STORE EMPLOYEES GET PAID TO DO.

I'm not kidding.

...

Still here? All right, hand the twenty to the cashier, head home, find a comfy spot and let's see if I can't get through this, shall we? Don't even wait for the cashier to hand you any change, you're going to need to absorb bigger punishment than that to get through this book, much less your day job as an innovator.

So, what's this book going to be about? Well, first we're going to spend some time trying to clarify exactly what kind of Innovator we're talking about here. We're not talking about the guys who come up with the cutting-edge tech inventions you see at CNES each year. No, we're talking about people who go about their job with inspiration, risk-taking, progressive thinking and more. They ask themselves: "Is this how it ought to be?" We're talking about the thousands of *you* that I've spoken to over the years who have ideas on how to make things better at your jobs and at your companies, and the risks that come to *you* by going off-plan and getting things done in a different way.

Then, we're going to turn that around and talk about them. Yeah – *them*! They are the 'theys' that will surround and outnumber you in your organization. There's more them than we, and those who are them are quite powerful. You might not even like them. But, learning about *them* prepares *you* for the game, so we'd best dive in.

We'll talk about why you should bother. Innovators tend to be as ambitious as anybody, so how does this act of 'innovating' fit into a career plan? And, what more are you going to have to do that others who take a more traditional career-building approach will not?

We'll get into timelines & tools. All projects are bumpy by nature[1], but there are key differences between Innovation efforts and the work being done by people going a more traditional route. For example, innovators are often surprised to get to the end of the effort, to the point of clear success, only to see the same nay-sayers and doubters continuing to cheer against you. So, before you begin this journey, you're going to want a few items in your arsenal that will help you survive the ups-and-downs.

We'll talk about *how* to actually be successful in your efforts. Sure, I'd prefer to stay theoretical and expound on all the things I've learned and know (I love to listen to *me*!), but I can see in your eyes that you want actual, practical advice about what *you* should do. So there you go, fine, look what you made me do.

We'll also dig into the type of obstacles only Innovators will face during your projects, including how to anticipate those obstacles and how to 'save face' through what will be some trying times.

---

[1] Bumpy by Nature would, incidentally, be a great name for a band, if any of you want to bail *right here* and go and do something more practical for a living.

We also describe how large companies are absolutely the *worst* place for innovation – not because they have to be, but because nobody will bother to fix the problems big companies have even if we tell you exactly how.

Throughout the book we'll also share excerpts from interviews I've done with Innovative leaders. These leaders come from different industries, different size companies, public and private firms and at different points in their careers. I think you'll find some of what they have to say familiar, candid and relatable.

Through it all, I'm going to try to have fun with you. Yes, this book covers a serious subject ... but I think a lot of the situations you have to overcome as an innovator are undeniably absurd, so we may as well call a duck a duck and see the crazy side of it. Sounds right to me.

But, enough! Let's get this started!

SECTION ONE: WE TRY TO UNDERSTAND INNOVATION

In this section of the book, we're going to dig into the psychology of Innovation from every angle – companies, leaders, teams and innovators.   We're going to try to understand: Why is this so hard?   What are you really facing?

I'm going to talk about:

1) What I specifically mean by innovation
2) Why large companies are not breeding grounds for innovation
3) Why you, personally, are the odd person to even *try* being innovative!

CHAPTER ONE: SERIOUSLY, THOUGH: ARE YOU *SURE*?

(Or, this could really *suck*)

Well, in spite of my best warnings, you kept going! From here forward I need to get serious on what kind of person I'm specifically addressing in this book, and how this differs from the other 99% of the people you work with. If I do my job well, *most* of you will figure out this book is not, actually, for you. Go read the one about moving the cheese, or not moving that cheese, or whatever it was that was supposed to happen to cheese. No harm done if you leave now.

I say this because the act of 'innovation' is one that exposes people. If you're not going to follow their ideas, then it means you have to tell everybody what *your* idea is. And then the judging begins. So, innovation is an act of confidence, resilience and leadership all in one. It's not for everyone.

WHAT DO I MEAN BY INNOVATION?

Before we can get too far, I really need to make sure we're on the same page of what I mean when I use the word Innovator. The word gets thrown around a lot, because it's useful in many different settings.

Let's start with the purest sense of the word. There are people who want to use the word Innovation in a business setting only when it comes to inventing new things or being on the 'cutting edge' of industry. Many, many companies these days are creating Innovation Centers or Strategy Teams within their organization to do the research and design work necessary to build new products or to start-up new business lines. Those people are impressive. I am not, exactly, talking to that group. They may indeed find helpful things in this book, as there is a *lot* of overlap between the problems they will run into and the problems you (my faithful reader) will encounter, but I'm not really addressing start-up or skunk works projects specifically.

Rather, the term Innovation in the context used throughout this book should refer to situations where you have people who tackle teams, companies and situations where they will hear the words: "That's not how we do it." These innovators are spread all over your company and they're frustrated, confused, flustered and often angry. They need to know how to push their ideas forward because they desperately want to make an impact. These are the people I'm talking to.

INNOVATION VS. OPTIMIZING

I think it's easier to start with a concept like 'Optimizing' than it is to dive straight into innovation. Great companies are chock-full of people who are good at improving and enhancing the routinely tracked products, services & processes of the company. Do you have a Supply Chain that has too much inventory at any given time? Somebody can fix that. Do you have a checkout process on your web page that asks too many questions and causes your customer to abandon the basket? Somebody can fix that. Do you need to find a way to squeeze another 2% productivity out of your workforce to offset wage growth? Somebody can fix that, too!

This 'optimizing' is not easy work by any means – it requires very talented and experienced people who understand not only the entirety of your product and process, but also have a decent understanding of your organization and how things work. I think the easiest analogy is to imagine you work at a manufacturing plant, one with a complex machine that transforms basic components into your final product. Great optimizers are able to spot when the machine is working slowly. They narrow down the causes of that slow-down so they can take action. They've seen the problems the machine can have so many times that they've formed a genuine intuition about it, something that's marvelous for your organization when it comes to maximizing throughput and keeping the machine running.

They're also great at describing what would make the machine work better – what parts need replacing, where your bottle-necks emerge, etc. When you get in a pinch and need to go max-throughput for a stretch, they know what corners can be temporarily cut without suffering any short-term damage to the machine (or product).

Experts in optimization think they *are* innovators! They correlate the effort and incremental leaps that they are required to exert with the struggles of innovation. However, there is a key distinction that I see in these two processes, specifically: how much resistance one receives in the pursuit of these leaps.

For example, let's say my company is in the business of making athletic shoes. One of my Machine Chiefs comes along and says that with a $2 million investment to upgrade a bottle-neck in the machine we can triple throughput of shoe production. In this situation, I understand implicitly that the business case for that idea is probably going to be a good one. The idea fits with what I do (make shoes), how I already do it (with the machine) and what I already want (more money). I probably have capital set aside each year for machine improvements and I have high expectations for annual throughput improvement. I more than likely have a team of people in Finance and Engineering whose jobs are to collect these ideas – often from the Machine Chiefs directly – and assess & implement the best ideas.

So, while this is a *great* idea and (probably) won't come easily, people automatically know their roles and know the process that can be followed to implement the idea.

Innovators have none of this luxury. Imagine if the same machine idea, above, came from an HR Generalist. On that basis alone, its likelihood of success grows murkier. Now imagine that the HR Generalist instead came up with an idea for a different use entirely for the machine, or even a different use for the Machine Chief. Heck, imagine that the HR Generalist just came up with a different *process* by which these throughput improvement ideas should be solicited and reviewed each year. That alone could be difficult!

You might agree and ask: Why is the idea coming from an HR Generalist at all? That's absurd! Stick to your job, HR flunkey![2] But in a perfect world, that is exactly the kind of organization you want, isn't it? One where every member of the organization is focused on the successful operation at the core of your business and how to improve it.

These are the people I'm trying to help.

SO, WHY IS BEING AN INNOVATOR A PROBLEM?

Imagine for a moment you've stumbled upon something brilliant. It's an idea, a product, an approach … whatever. But it's REAL

---

[2] Calm down. Jeez.

and it's PERFECT. That said, it's not familiar. You're going to have to do some selling, but how hard could this be – this idea/product/approach is SO GOOD! Right? In your mind, you're spending your promotion dollars already.

This is often where I share the Money Button metaphor.

THE MONEY BUTTON DILEMMA

You have gathered the 10 members of your company's executive leadership team together in your office. When all is quiet, you point to something new, and odd, affixed to your wall. You start:

"This is my new innovation for Our Great Company, which I call The Money Button. This button, when pressed, will cause my ceiling to open up and $10,000 cash to rain down upon us. This money is completely legal and tax-free. We can press The Money Button as often as we'd like – 24 hours a day, 7 days a week. It will never break down or need repair. And, we can use those funds for whatever we'd like – investment, dividends, bonuses or anything."

Here is where you wait for applause. It ain't coming.

In my experience, 9 of those 10 leaders are about to destroy your illusions. "Wait," one will say. "That button does not look like it came from our button procurement department. We have a strict contract with Buttons R' Us. That non-standard button is going to get us a $25 fine!"

"I agree," another will say. "And the color of the button is blue. Our research says our customers prefer red." (Note that you will try to interject here to remind them the button will never be seen or used by a customer, as this is an internal-only tool. This will not be heard and you will be accused of not putting the customer first.)

"Why is the button in *your* office?" another will say. "That's a long way for us to have to walk. If it were in the HR area, we could staff it more easily."

"That's another problem!" an industrious leader will quickly add. "We're up against tight budgets as it is. And all of this money is floating down in small bills, scattered all over the floor. There's no way we have the funds to staff the clean-up effort. This is a disaster!"

"Why wasn't I brought into The Money Button project earlier?" you'll hear, before turning to face a very stern expression from somebody who is clearly deeply disappointed in you. "This is exactly the sort of thing the Strategy Department should have been involved with. We could have avoided all these problems people are bringing up!"

And on-and-on it will go. And the sad thing is, as absurd as I've tried to make this story, many of you reading this right now are nodding along because you've seen this exact scenario play out in your company. To you, it doesn't seem crazy at all!

My point is: If the Money Button can't win universal acclaim from your organization, why do you think *your* *obviously* flawed idea will be embraced? Instead, you should be preparing for the opposite and making it part of your project to account for the resistance you're going to feel. Let me repeat that: Your PLAN should be to face resistance and overcome it, no matter how good you think your idea might be.

WHY WON'T PEOPLE TAKE THIS GIANT BAG OF MONEY I'M OFFERING THEM?

They don't see it that way. It's not because they're bad people or even bad at recognizing a good idea. In fact, I'm about to say something that I'm sure I'll repeat again in this book: In my 25 years working in large companies, I have never run into a sociopath. By sociopath, I mean somebody who is intentionally acting against their own (or others') best interests. So, if that's the case, why do many people work against your ideas?

Chapter Two dives into this more completely, but let me start with two huge institutional roadblocks that exist at a number of corporations. In those companies, a large percentage of the people who have been promoted up the ranks over the years are those who contributed successfully to the company's growth. They got those opportunities because they were good business people, sure … but there were also amazing studies of the organization's culture. And, probably, they learned two critical lessons in their own career journeys:

1. Model yourself after others: You will often hear leaders give advice like "The CEO doesn't like this particular phrase" or "My boss will never go for it – we tried this

years ago and he vomited all over it." Many leaders in large organizations are very quick studies of conformity – what does this culture accept? What does it reject? What are 'keys to success'? What battles aren't worth fighting? Who's vulnerable? What perspectives (or turns of phrase) resonate with others and give me power, versus those that don't?

I personally worked for a company where a simple and powerful attack on character was to question another employee's 'partnership', or to accuse them of having 'sharp elbows'. Sailing on your own for any type of work simply wasn't permissible. Alternatively, starting a presentation by showing how many people you'd taken as 'partners' was automatically admired.

This kind of group think does not correlate to efficient behaviors. I'm not suggesting that 'taking partners' is a bad idea, but the fact that simply talking about your partners was a tactic that was so easily deployed and overtly welcomed is indicative of a culture that rewards mimicking itself. And that culture, by definition, cannot reward alternative approaches.

2. <u>Standardize development</u>: The next wave of leaders in big companies are most often chosen by the current group of leaders. Except, of course, in bloody coups, but let's assume your company has not reached this point[3].

   In small companies with fewer overall people and fewer management layers, up-and-coming talent gets more

---

[3] Yet.

personal apprenticeship from its leaders, often able to watch and learn from them directly. In turn, those leaders can personally observe if the up-and-coming talent has all the attributes it will take to be successful in higher roles.

As companies get bigger, there is less time for leaders to individually develop talent and more of a need to broadly communicate things like 'values' and 'career building'. So leaders turn to delegates, particularly mid-level management, to deliver these messages. That's where things start to go wrong …

Because, as well-intentioned delegate #1 goes about developing this communication, he or she knows it would be absolutely crass to just say the words: "To get ahead, you should make heaping gobs of money for the mothership". Hell, No! Delegate #1 didn't go to business school for four years just to resort to using plain language! "I gotta *business* that shit up," he or she says.

So, those words get softened down to horoscope–level generic skills like 'Delivers Results' or 'Optimizes Relationships'. Messages like 'Try Not to Be a Jerk' get changed to 'Have Fun at Work!', which I appreciate but may or may not have the intended outcome.

Is it any wonder people get confused?

The point being: On that day when the CEO or SVP goes on a rant about how slowly the organization is moving toward the new goals or initiatives she designed, one of the key questions leaders should ask is: Are we truly championing and rewarding the *preferred* behaviors?

WHAT DOES THIS MEAN FOR YOU?

The act of 'going your own way' (albeit reasonably & effectively) isn't going to sit right with many of you. As humans, we naturally seek approval and a feeling of fitting-in - maybe not in our moment-to-moment actions but, in general, we do like to feel comfortable. We understand that the path to success is not often achieved via 'upsetting the people around us'. Even our parents rewarded us if we behaved how they *wanted* us to, which was often how *they* behaved.

Being an innovator will often feel like the opposite of all that. You will frequently wonder where this path leads, career-wise (exactly the reason we wrote Chapter Eight) because, *if* successful, it will no longer be on that simple track upward on the carefully-constructed organizational ladder that leads from accountant to senior accountant to Lord-High of All Accountants[4] to CFO. You are now on a path that looks a lot more like a mountain goat leaping from one pebble-strewn outcropping to another.

That's why this will feel bad – it's a strange career choice, an odd way of proceeding in general, and a mystery to those around you. Have I convinced you yet to be an Innovator?

---

[4] Admission: I may not understand Accounting career paths very well

EXCERPTS FROM AN INTERVIEW
"TONYA", CIO[ii]

Tonya worked at a very large retailer before moving to be CIO at a $1 Billion-plus CPG for two years. She has since moved on again to join one of the world's largest private companies.

The CPG company was aware of Tonya's very different approach to supporting the business and consciously brought her in to make changes to the IT function, for which they were not satisfied with historical support or results.

As you'll see, even the best intentions may not always be enough!

Excerpts:

TONYA: The IT area was a total back-office function [when I arrived at the CPG].   The CEO said to me, "We spend more money on IT than any other function at our organization and we get the least amount of value out of it."   So, that was the CEO's perspective and that's how the team was treated.

ME: Good to know.

TONYA: The team was scared.   They couldn't have their own opinion, they would just get squashed and … sort of shamed.   So, they were super-thrilled that somebody coming in at the level I was coming in … it was going to put them on the map.

ME: Sure.

TONYA: I spent the first 60 days assessing [things], and learned that this team is not going to cut it. There were about 30 employees. They had outsourced all of this crap that didn't need to be out-sourced, and it was just a total ... no value. Didn't have sense of budget, forecast or value proposition for the dollars we were spending. All of those were indications that these weren't the right leaders. So, a team of 30 people ... I started there in June, and by mid-October 6 of them were gone.

ME: Wow.

TONYA: It was unbelievably painful. These people operated like a family. They would go to each other's children's birthday parties, they had worked really tough times together. And then here's this, you know ...

ME: Yes.

TONYA: "Who is she, we don't know her ... and she has just fired our senior leadership." And I told you, that was one of the most stressful parts of my career. Because of the personal responsibility of that, and then just absorbing everybody's feelings and responses and reactions –

ME: You owned that decision and that direction forward. In part it made you a *leader* because you were making decisions. It's the hardest part ... you know many people start their careers and say "I want to be that leader" but they don't appreciate how painful that job is. Because you are alone.

TONYA: Totally alone.

ME: I need to do this, but nobody's going to throw me a parade.

TONYA: I think the guys in the executive committee were impressed that I had come in and in such a short period of time had made this happen. They were super supportive of it. But I was ultimately doing it by myself. And I was not accustomed to having that much responsibility without a peer group that you know is going to support you through it. There was nobody! It was a very lonely experience.

■■

TONYA: I spent a lot of time studying the culture and not only the conversations I had but also what did we communicate as a leadership team. We communicated these values. We communicated our goals and our strategic priorities. But then the actions of the leaders that I saw were not in concert with that.

ME: You've talked before about these disconnects.

TONYA: There was a lot of fear. It was a real fear-based culture. The CEO has all the power. Everybody is his minion. And if they have to go up against him in any way, they will just back down. So, they'll say [what their priorities are], but then if the action needs to be approved by the CEO, they will back down.

ME: Fascinating.

TONYA: So, after a while, you start to see patterns. You *say* you want to do these things, but you don't *really* want to do it, especially if it will involve a really hard upward communication. We'll just back down. And, eventually, I don't want to be a part of that.

■■

CHAPTER TWO: Big companies are *supposed* to fail

(Or, a rant about large-ness and why it's within the very nature of big companies to snuff out innovation and destroy the souls of its employees)

In Chapter 1 we covered what innovation is, at least for purposes of this book. In Chapter 2, I want to help you understand why this journey of innovation – whether it is for one particular project or perhaps an entire career path – is so difficult for even the most talented leader. I'm going to talk about the resistance you will feel, the *organizational psychology* that makes big companies so resistant to new ideas. The better you understand this psychology of organizations and how it comes to be, the better your chances of success as an innovator who may test that structure.

The reasons innovators struggle at large companies include:

1) Large companies are very much like living organisms, with defensive systems designed to seek out and stop risky behavior (which is what true innovation can often seem to be);

2) The very act of growth in large companies creates myopic cultures that *effectively* discourage innovation and innovators from existing in the first place;

3) At exactly the time when leaders should be looking to new ideas to help re-ignite growth, they will instead

instinctively double-down on 'what's worked before', because that's what they know how to do

4) There will *always* be some part of your business that is not running optimally, which will continue to get leadership's focus and drive them crazy (right when they *should* be working on transformational new ideas);

5) Large companies are rife with mis-incentives that can block new ideas from getting traction;

6) The diversity of leadership and talent required to sustain innovation is *still* not understood well enough to be valued by senior leadership in large companies.

BIG COMPANIES WILL, EVENTUALLY, DISAPPEAR

Wait, what? Is that correct? *Do* big companies tend to fail? After all, companies like Exxon, General Electric, General Motors, Boeing, Proctor & Gamble, General Mills, IBM, Caterpillar and more littered the Fortune 500 all the way back in 1955 and are still there today.

True! Unfortunately, for every company I can name from the Fortune 500 list in 1955 that's still alive today, I can name 3 others you won't even recognize: Esmark, Navistar, Borden Chemical, Wilson, Bendix, Ryerson Tull, AMAX, Olin, Allis-Chalmers, Anaconda, Cudahy, Kennecott, NL Industries, Sealed Air, BorgWarner, Avco, Pure Oil, Amstar and more have long since been absorbed, radically devalued or outright shuttered in the last 60 years[iii]. And those are just the names I plucked from the Top 100 companies in the U.S. at that time!

In fact, let's look at this chart, adopted from the excellent work of the Ewing Marion Kaufmann Foundation in 2012[iv]:

CHART 2.1

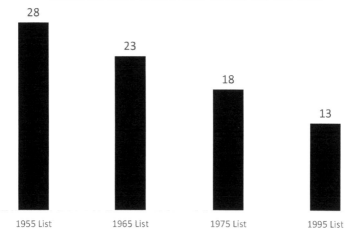

How Many Years Did it Take for Half the Companies Listed on the Fortune 500 to Fall Off the List?

Simply put, Chart 2.1 shows that the companies listed on the Fortune 500 list in any given past decade (1955, 1965, 1975 or 1995) are turning over at a rapidly *increasing* rate. In other words, while it took nearly 30 years for *half* of the companies on the 1955 Fortune 500 list to fall off, that turnover rate was down to about 13 years by 1995!

This isn't just about the very biggest firms, either. The Kaufmann report goes on to state that "of the firms listed on the NY Stock Exchange in 1925 only 13% existed in their independent corporate form in 2004." Said differently, 87% do *not* exist!

So the point that I'm asking you concede here is pretty straight-forward: over an extended period, the majority of large companies *at least* taper-off to relative irrelevancy … with the *vast* majority going so far as to reach complete insolvency.

So the interesting question is 'Why do these firms, who have the very best of resources, talent and financial advantages, ultimately prove unable to sustain themselves?'

THE COMPANY AS AN ORGANISM

Why do all companies eventually disappear?

One of the key arguments I am going to make in this book is that companies are more like living organisms than people initially realize. They are born, they live, they are able to reproduce[5], they have immunization systems to defend themselves, and they die. The better you understand this organism, the better your chances of success.

If you, my prospective innovator-in-chief, were to be walking across a grassy field and run into a snake, there are certain instincts that would take over. Even if you were the type of person so bold as to say, "I am going to walk over and pat that snake on the head,", your body would still be on-guard. You would recognize that the animal you're approaching can hurt you, even though you intend it no harm. You will alter your approach and heighten your senses – completely instinctively – for this reason.

But for so many of you there is a lack of understanding that the corporate organism you're approaching *also* has life to it. It has defense mechanisms set up to defend it. When you bring your

---

[5] Ew. But, seriously, I mean that large companies have a tendency to spin off new companies, and also are often providers of crucial angel funding for start-ups that would have failed without them.

new approaches and new thinking to the table, so many of you do so naively because you don't understand the reaction you're going to get. You don't understand the creature – you just want your chance to pat it on the head.

So why do it at all? Why take the chances? Because, as I've said, the corporation is alive … and like all living creatures, it must continue to grow and evolve or it will die. This is true throughout nature, and it's no different for corporate America. Without change and adaptation, the animal will die. And, without people like you to make the attempt, the changes your company needs will never occur.

Plus, fuck it – it's fun! But let's get educated before we make the attempt, just to be safer. That's why we have to truly understand the lifespan of a company.

THE LIFE AND CURSE OF GETTING 'BIG'

So, let's start with a relatively simple premise about the lifespan of a large company. To represent this, I'm going to draw a curved graph as such:

CHART 2.2

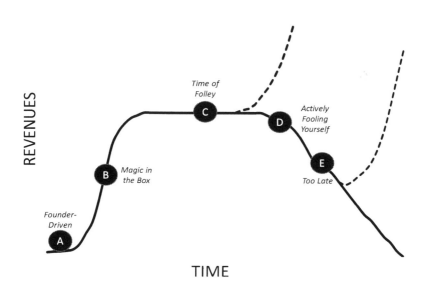

This curve – or, at least, the solid line within - represents the expected life of your typical giant corporation. It is born, grows, reaches a plateau and eventually starts to fade.

There are several pieces to Chart 2.2 worth calling out. First, the rise of your typical giant corporation (the timeframe during which Point B occurs) is much faster than a lot of people realize – many companies go from 'startup' to 'uber-relevant' (if not 'massive') in a very small amount of time, maybe just over a decade. Microsoft in 1980 was a brand known only to the computer-savvy, hidden behind a piece of software called MS-DOS. By 1990, Windows had become the dominant platform on computer systems. In 1995

Netflix didn't exist, by 2015 it was the dominant streaming video brand. In 1995 Target was a hip subsidiary of the Dayton Hudson Corporation. By 2004 Dayton's and Marshall Field's were being sold away to make room for the Target juggernaut beneath. That's not to say that these companies stopped growing after a decade, but merely to represent that the typical rise of a substantial corporation happens very fast.

Why is that? I'll get myself into trouble here, but I have a 3-pronged theory that attempts to explain it:

1) A great leader (or vision)
2) *Tremendous* luck
3) Fortuitous timing

Of these, the least important is the leader. Now, I *do* think a Jeff Bezos or Sergey Brin or Ray Kroc or Sam Walton matter. The act of getting past that first very early curve in my graph (point A) is crucially driven by relentless passion, clear vision and a tolerance for risk that few people can tolerate. Most start-ups do fail, after all. So, I acknowledge the indispensable role these leaders play, at least in survival, but …

I find myself unable to dismiss the second two factors: luck and timing. How much did IBM's rise to prominence benefit from the space race in the 60's? How much did Microsoft benefit (rather than cause, as it might claim) the miniaturization of computers that started in the late 70's? How much did Target benefit from the boom-years of the middle class during the Clinton era? These companies and their products certainly capitalized on those opportunities, which was no small feat … but when those opportunities changed or disappeared, so (often) did the fortunes of these companies.

By Point B in Chart 2.2, the company is now rapidly growing and thriving. A lot of hard work is happening during this phase, and that work is being done by incredibly smart people. However, the very early phases of this upward tick mean that the product has proven itself valuable, timely and relevant in the market. Yes - the people involved are important because of their ability to sustain that growth model and to squeeze performance out of this operating model during a crucial period of its life. However, the company is NOT growing *because* of them, specifically. If every single one of those people were replaced by somebody of (relatively) equal experience, the company would still do very, very well ... because the *idea* the company is built upon is right and the *timing* is right. The business wants to expand and (obviously) the market wants this, too. It's intangible & amazing, the very definition of 'lightning in a bottle'.

But because of human nature, this eventually creates a problem. Inevitably, the people involved do attribute the success of the business to themselves. Some might call it arrogance, but I'd describe it much closer to 'extreme confidence'. As an employee in today's corporate environment (and I'd say this is true at most all companies), you spend so much time explaining the value you're adding, if only to justify your latest annual performance review, bonus or promotion, that inevitably you come to at least largely believe that those sales gains, margin improvements or whatever wouldn't have happened without *you*. I want to emphasize: there's nothing evil or misguided about any of this, it's just how human beings are. And so much of what happens next, both to the company *and* how it impacts your ability to be innovative at that company, stem from this reality.

So, this is the first[6] time in this book where I will make this point: If you go about your career expecting and understanding that most people you run into will act and behave like the human beings they

---

[6] But far from last. I will drive you crazy with this point by the end of this book.

are, instead of some idealized version of 'leadership' you might hope they would be, you have a fighting chance at being really, really successful at your pursuits. Conversely, the more you are surprised by this reality, the more frustrated you will become.

THE INEVITABLE INTRANSIGENCE OF BEING BIG

By Point C of Chart 2.2, let's say 15-25 years or so into that cycle, the growth model begins to taper off. This could happen for many reasons. Perhaps you've simply hit the upper thresholds of the market (everybody has an iPad, and they don't have to be replaced that often). Perhaps competitors have entered your market. Or, your physical assets have aged to the point where marginal growth can't be supported by your base without further expansion or asset refresh, which you can't truly afford. Doesn't matter – the only point is that the company has reached that point where growth has slowed considerably, if not stalled altogether.

But, much more is happening to your company underneath the surface at Point C. In this phase, many companies are actually realizing they are now 'big'. They are building out infrastructure, like a corporate office building, a dedicated payroll department, building systems to automate routine work, etc. They've expanded their HR teams to handle the problems of being big – increased hiring, increased firing, succession planning, leadership training & development, and more. The *details* are starting to matter as much as the big picture:

- PowerPoint decks and presentations to management are expected to be more refined; after all, we're ACME Inc, dammit!

- More meetings are happening, especially 'staff' meetings, to the point where even lowest-level employees have busy calendars
- Routine processes, like Annual Performance Reviews, start to take on importance, because there are now people who are in charge of those processes and can enforce compliance. Leaders and teams get in trouble when they're not turned in on time, so more time and energy is devoted by leaders just to stay out of trouble.
- Lawyers are reviewing each case before an employee is fired, causing more timid managers to avoid taking any performance actions whatsoever
- Your pockets are now big enough that the company is getting sued more frequently, which means internal audit, corporate safety and other teams begin to emerge and institute rules to safe-guard your assets.
- Budgeting and budget processes get complicated, often requiring weeks or months of executives' time
- Best practices are starting to get documented, and with them comes training time requirements
- Your 'culture' is being studied and refined by people who are tasked with those activities, so it can be taught and adhered to ("At this company, we keep costs low by using our pencils until no more than 2.25 inches remain in the stub")
- And on, and on …

The need for the creation and monitoring of these details creates more need for headcount, in turn creating even *greater* capacity within the organization for devotion to detail and just, generally, more work overall … work that is largely tangential to, but not specific to, the effort that got you through Points A and B on Chart 2.2. In other words, there's a lot more work being done at your company that doesn't directly create growth or profit, but is being rationalized as important for the perceived health and sustainability of the *company*[7], not to drive the business. And that's when you *know* you're big – when you find that you have people devoted to the care & feeding of the company itself! I told you big companies were animals!

It goes without saying that the more of each employee's time devoted to working on the business of *being* a business, and the less time spent on the actions of making that business thrive, the harder it's going to be to change things when you reach Point C. This is your first big hurdle as an innovator – how will you get the company to overcome its addiction to 'corporate process' so it can focus on renewed growth? At least some of you who are reading this today are working for a company that is *actively* failing, but will still allow itself to lose weeks or months of its team's productivity to do processes like budget building, annual performance reviews or the like.

THE CURSE OF 'SQUEEZING MORE'

There is another subtle influence emerging in your company at Point C in Chart 2.2. It is now true that most of the leaders of your much bigger organization are those that were growing up in your firm during Point B – the ones who rode that wave of growth to greater opportunity, promotion and status. These people are smart, and deserving, of their success.

As we established earlier in this chapter, those leaders naturally attribute the prior successes of the company with their own historical actions, approaches and strategies. Then, as the company expanded and its resources grew, those leaders became

---

[7] Specifically, the HQ portion of the company

instrumental in engineering and standardizing the processes used to run the business, in building the tools and reporting that are used to monitor it, and in crafting the strategies that will take advantage of those processes and tools to improve business results. In other words, they engineered their divisions / pyramids / organizations to align their team's efforts in the way that the leader believed was optimal ... largely because that's how *they* did the work.

This leads to the following:

1) It takes so much time and effort to get these initial processes and tools created, that the requirement to *follow* these exact processes becomes institutionalized. People who perfect those efforts are rewarded. Group-think emerges about how to be effective.

2) It also becomes normal to not listen to outside voices and ideas, because they have not 'earned' the right to provide those ideas. Those voices are weeded out. So, those people are simply not there when new ideas are needed later.

3) Inevitably, when problems occur and financial plans start being missed, leaders and their teams double-down on the existing way of doing things. They believe the answers must be in the data and processes they are already using. If something is wrong, somebody must be *doing* something wrong, and if we can find and correct that 'something', we will turn the course.

4) Because no system in any company is ever being run perfectly, the leaders and their teams *will* find areas of their operation that could be improved, thereby validating

their beliefs from point #3, above. They will throw resources at correcting those problems. This is a cycle that may *never* end, because (as I said) there will always be things that aren't running perfectly.

5) Because everybody is working on 'fixing the glitches', nobody is working on new ideas and strategies.

6) And, so the vicious circle begins.

The problems inherent with all of this are subtle, but crucial. One is that the returns-on-time-invested by these leaders on fixing glitches can be very small and short-term in nature. The second problem is that if you, the innovator, are trying to assist these leaders with righting their ship, you may find yourself 'walled off' from the team you're trying to help, because anything other than doubling-down on the current processes is not being accepted. You will be branded 'off-priority' and your bosses will be told that you are 'distracting the team'.

No company ever reaches the phase where it squeezes *all* the value from its assets. There are always additional efficiencies to be gained in production, costs that can be reduced from vendors, prices that can be optimized, new markets to reach, new marketing programs to try. There is always profit and growth possible from where you are today and those opportunities should *not* be ignored. But no company – I will say *zero* of them – will ever see themselves re-start a growth phase because of these efforts. So, when you are at Point C, leaders must ensure their organizations are matching the effort you're putting toward Optimization with the effort you're putting toward Innovation. In most companies at Point C, this is simply not going to be true. It's not in leadership's makeup.

I can't say this enough: every tendency I'm describing here represents the natural actions and reactions of human beings. If you have spent 15 years turning Blockbuster Video from a regional VHS rental store into a powerhouse of revenue *so great it can impact the types of movies that studios make* ... the temptation to continue to tweak and adapt that bricks-and-mortar model and to reenergize your business in the face of new competition are understandable, logical, rational and human. They are, unfortunately, sub-optimal. With almost no exception, the assets and utility you've ridden to Point C in Chart 2.2 will never again yield growth of the kind you've experienced before. To get back to growth, something new must happen, and the question must be asked in that situation: who is going to drive that for you, and how?

UH, OH!

Point D in Chart 2.2 is interesting in its own right. Here, now, you've reached a moment where all growth has stopped and, with rare exception, your firm is experiencing declines for the first time in its existence. I've labeled this timing 'Actively Fooling Yourself' because these results are almost always ignored or minimized by the company, the leaders, the Board and more. The initial negative results are rationalized away via the economy, weather patterns and whatever else is handy. These rationalizations are almost always perceived as forces *external* to the company.

And all of that often leads to Point E, which is where it is simply too late for a turnaround. Even if the market has changed or new ideas have arisen, for these companies it's not feasible to execute. Capital has dried up. The 'big bets' of the past years have caused you to absorb too much debt.   The bank simply won't let you do it.   Whatever.

In my research, very, very few companies make it to the dotted upward-curving line after Point E.   Apple is probably the single most notorious example of it, but there are (a few) others in the last 100 years who've done the same kind of turnaround.

And, that's it.   You'll notice I didn't put a Point F on Chart 2.2, because why bother?   I'll leave that shit for completists – I'm trying to help people who can still be helped.

THERE IS A MIS-INCENTIVES PROBLEM

So – *how* do companies break out of these binds and become the kind of organizations that move back along either of the 2 upward-sloping dotted lines in Chart 2.2?   And, how does all of this relate to your job as an innovator?

First of all, let me be clear: if you're fortunate enough to have a good job in a big corporation, you are 99.99% surrounded by uber-rational people.   From the very highest to the very lowest[8] people in the organization, they will behave in a predictable manner to predictable stimuli.   You can succeed if you can understand, anticipate and influence these stimuli.

So, you can do this.   But the key to success may be harder than most people want to accept, and that is: fundamentally, on a very basic-and-core level, you need to expect people to act like 'people'.   Said differently, are you the kind of person who gets very frustrated when somebody in traffic cuts you off, or tailgates,

---

[8] "Lowest" could probably be worded better, huh?   You, uh … you get what I mean.

or merges without a blinker? If so, this is going to be hard, because the reality is that while you may be a wonderful driver with impeccable defensive maneuvering skills, society is filled with those who are not. They don't value it. They value that tight little space right in front of you RIGHT NOW in YOUR LANE. They assume if they use their blinker you'll inch up and crowd the car in front of you and make that space unavailable for them, because THAT'S WHAT THEY WOULD DO. Would things be better if all people adhered to all best traffic practices? Maybe! But I'm not living in that world, so I deal with the one we've got. And that's the world we're here to try to help you navigate as an innovator.

In our real world, different people behave in very different ways … but you can always trace their choices, behaviors, trigger points, attention span and more back to specific incentives.

Unfortunately, big companies provide mis-incentives to their employees all – the – time. Constantly. We get into it more in Chapter Three, but for now here are some examples to chew on:

- Many companies have a rigid do-not-exceed-budget rule. Executive leaders, of course, expect their middle managers to understand that going $10,000 over budget to support an idea that will generate multi-millions in sales would be very justifiable. Instead – and I *promise* you, this will happen - a culture grows of extremely competent budget-checkers (paid in the $200k-per-year range, often enough). They're not looking for opportunity, they're ensuring their budget is met! No shareholder has benefitted from this, but it *is* rational.

- Companies get their severance programs wrong because they try to be cheap. Progress involves risk. Risk involves the chances of being fired. Outside of outright incompetence, taking risks and failing should be rewarded with a substantial severance, the kind that will not (by reputation alone) impede risk-taking elsewhere in your firm. Otherwise, your team and leaders can do math and will understand that the returns from 'keeping the ship afloat' and not rocking that boat are crucial to their family and retirement plans. Eventually, they will stop taking risks … especially right at that later time in their careers when the know the most, know where the biggest returns can be found and are most equipped to go and get those returns.

- Understandably, most companies are set-up to assess their performance based on Last Year. How did you change versus last year? Well, what if last year doesn't align with where the company is going? For example, if you are trying to sell New Product X, than growth in Old Product Y doesn't reflect the company's intentions. Don't get me wrong – the cash flows from Old Product Y are probably appreciated – but did you move the needle toward the future of the company? Probably not – in fact, you may have hindered it significantly.

- The 'too much' problem – companies are terrible at choosing a few key initiatives and throwing their resources behind it. By allowing too many different priorities to exist – sometimes dozens of them for each Pyramid of your organization – you are causing three problems. The first is that by having too many priorities, you decrease the likelihood of any of them being accomplished satisfactorily. Second is that you increase the odds of conflicting priorities existing across pyramids – for example, 'controlling headcount' in HR being counter to 'hiring for the new sales team' in Merchandising. Finally, you have provided a built-in excuse to anybody who cannot complete one of your priorities. If you say, "I told you that I wanted the new Sales team up-and-running by May –

you're delaying the launch of our new product!", they can just reply "I wanted to do that, but I had to dedicate my team's time to the rollout of the new ERP system, which you told us needed to be completed by April." As a leader you should never *provide* built-in excuses to your organization.

These are all things – and there are many more – that will keep your organization from truly taking action when change needs to be made, especially at crucial points where clear new direction needs to be taken. The reality is: Incentives, both financial and otherwise, will curb your ability to make those changes.

You, as the innovator I am educating in this book, *must* understand the power of incentives *and* mis-incentives over people. You *must* understand how to find this information out about people. You *must* understand when those incentives need to be changed, and how to do that. Incentives are the single biggest driver of companies being inert, and the single biggest spark that can change that reality.

And those incentives are *not* always financial. We'll cover some of that in Chapter Three.

WE ALL WISH WE COULD BE LIKE THE COOL KIDS

As I've said[9], organizations are supposed to fail. And, part of why they will is because you are not truly developing the next generation of leaders in a way that can take advantage of the new ideas and approaches they might bring. In fact, you are most likely developing them in just the opposite way.

---

[9] Waaaaay back at the beginning of this Chapter. Remember that? It was a while ago, huh?

Think back – when you were fairly new in your career, you were trying to figure out how to succeed. At that time, a lot of 'success' was derived from getting accolades from your leaders, people who would tell you that you were either doing well or not. These people controlled your ability to get promoted. They were your role models for behavior and growth and controlled the keys to opportunity and wealth.

So, is it any surprise that so many of us end up dressing, thinking and behaving like the most influential leaders in our organization? If you look at the leadership team and they ubiquitously dress in the latest fashions, you will start to correlate dress with success. If the leadership team all has MBA's, you will define that as a milestone to future success. If every C-suite leader took a turn going out and running one of your stores, warehouses or manufacturing plants (to learn what life is like 'on the ground'), you will naturally want a chance to do so yourself.

Is this approach to homogenized development where your new ideas are supposed to come from?

Now, let me be clear – I am not saying that you're a fool to send that talented employee out to your warehouse for a year to get that experience. It can be invaluable. But is that 'the way'? Are there other paths to success available? At some companies, there are not – it has become the *rule* because that is how all the current leaders got to their position. It is no longer being scrutinized for importance, or checked to be sure there are alternatives available for people for whom that may not be an option.

Even if you do send talent out to the field for experience, what are you doing to augment that experience with efforts that will provoke them to think out of the box? Perhaps those field experiences should be coupled with major initiatives intended to improve or change operations, with your up-and-coming leaders in charge. The exercise should always be about the future needs of the company, not 'the way things have always been done'.

ANOTHER PROBLEM: LAWS vs. POLICIES vs. RULES

Here I'll be talking about addiction. Specifically, the addiction that companies have with their 'rules', and how those rules impact their ability to develop innovation.

Let's specify first what we mean by rules. I see three sources of restrictions within companies:

1. Laws – this should be very clear, as these are the laws of the federal government, your states and your cities. There may be laws handed down from controlling agencies to your specific businesses – for example, the FTC, SEC or otherwise. You need to follow the law!

2. Policies – these are created by companies and augment what the law has to say. They go above and beyond the law. These, too, are strict. And, they should not change all that often – good policies should be able to last for years.

3. Rules – these are created by companies and often have (or had) a point when created. These should be continuously questioned by leaders. I'm not saying they shouldn't be followed … but, boy, 'rules' are often lazy and dated.

Let's use some examples. The law says that we are not allowed to discriminate in our hiring practices based on gender, race or religion (amongst other things). This is unassailable. My company's policy says that the law does not go far enough and that we, as hiring managers, cannot discriminate on *anything* that is outside of the specific needs of the job itself. Therefore, while the law does not protect short people, ugly people or overweight people, the company says that none of those can be reasons for me to reject a candidate. This policy is excellent – I can never imagine a reason for it to change. Finally, my company has a 'rule' that every 90 days I need to attest, in writing, that I understand the policy and have not actually discriminated in my hiring practices for any reason. This rule is clearly stupid. It creates work for limited benefit. The company is obviously trying to limit its legal exposure while reminding you of the policies – it's the kind of nonsense corporate lawyers come up with when unchecked.

Laws and policies should be sacred and difficult to change. However, if you're like most companies, you probably have too damn many rules. Rules are typically a way to help low-level people avoid having to say 'no' to people – it allows them to simply quote the rules as a way of rejecting a request from their peers to help solve a problem!

I recently had a colleague share this story:

> *I work in the Financial Securities industry. My company has us fill out paperwork on new accounts. I got a new client who had four accounts that were transitioning over. There was only room on the form to list two accounts, and to have to fill out two forms would have required a *bunch* of redundant data entry on my part, so I called my home office to ask for help.*
>
> *The lady on the phone told me that, indeed, I needed to fill out two forms. I pointed out that this was a lot*

of redundant work. She said that corporate actually required that only *one* account could be listed per form, but that they'd already bent the rules so that we could do two accounts per form, so I should be happy about that!

Of course, being me, I immediately asked – "So, if we're already breaking the rules to put two account numbers on each form, why can't we just go further and put four accounts on the form?"

This company, even when they *think* they're breaking the rules, they're following them! This is not about the law, or about good policy to prevent abuse … this is just about following a set of rules put in place to steer the bureaucracy.

Question the rules! Test them! They are throttling your organization, I promise you. There should be processes[10] where stupid rules can easily get submitted up to leaders, particularly the CEO, for review. I think that person would be surprised how many dumb rules get forwarded her direction.

WHY DIVERSITY (OF THOUGHT) IS STILL A PROBLEM (AND HOW IT IMPACTS INNOVATION)

Unfortunately, when most corporate leaders are confronted with diversity as a challenge, they look at it purely as a question of racial and gender diversity. They understand, because they have been told, that diversity is good for thought leadership, team building and other aspects of running a good business, but let's

---

[10] One example process: The modern day 'suggestion box' for the CEO, except instead of suggestions make it an e-mail address where people can anonymously submit stupid rules they are forced to follow.

face it ... the only reason a conversation around diversity comes up at the C-suite is due to issues with a *lack* of racial or gender representation. In other words, it's presented as a metrics problem, not an opportunity.

So, I'm going to hit on valuable elements of diversity that aren't often considered, including:

1) Diversity of industry – your organization is a collection of assets (physical, intangible, intellectual, patent or otherwise) that have been brought together over time toward a common mission. These assets were purchased to enable your operations and to solve problems. You see them for what they are. Who, in your organization, gives you a chance to see those assets through a different lens? For example, if you own a series of industrial manufacturing locations through the United States, would somebody with a retail or e-commerce background perceive different uses for those buildings? Would their eyes light up at the chance to start a new product line or operation that you wouldn't ever have conceived?

2) Diversity of experience – One of the greatest dangers in business is confirmation bias, or the act of accidentally coming to interpret new evidence as reinforcing what you had believed all along. Are there people close to you who have been through corporate bankruptcies, or mergers, or experienced good-and-bad change management efforts? People who have a chance to call something out as 'troubling' that you may not have seen on your own? Does your leadership team have venues where these voices get to review data with them and share what they see & think?

3) Diversity of culture/geography – I was part of an organization that was extremely successful in the United States and decided to expand that operation to Canada. It did not go well. A bunch of very smart people radically under-estimated the differences in how that customer shopped. Do *you* have the thought leadership to help you identify and understand these cultural challenges and lead through them?

4) Diversity of tenure – more than likely your leadership team is comprised of people who have been with your company for a long time. Do new voices, even if they have to come from lower levels, get a chance to share insight or be heard? Do new voices get shunned into silence or are special steps taken so their voices are augmented?

I'm sure I'm missing many other types of diversity that could benefit you as a leader. The point is: all of these factors can influence your ability to either promote or stifle change in your organization. The culture you create, if it's one where you are hoping for innovative thought and leadership, ultimately stems from the diversity you crave and reinforce, and it's a much, much deeper opportunity (or problem) than what's represented in the simple diversity metrics most companies actually keep.

THE TAKE-AWAY

So, why have we spent so long on this? Because *you* need to understand the multiple & various forces at play inside large companies and how they can impact your efforts. You need to understand that people, however good, will *act like people* and *how* that comes to manifest itself inside large companies. All of this equips you for the mental aspects of what you're trying to do. Without it, you are literally walking up to the snake and petting it on the head without any idea of what to expect might happen and how you'll react.

EXCERPTS FROM AN INTERVIEW
"CATHY", COMPENSATION LEADER[v]

Cathy is a leader in the Compensation department of a Fortune 500 public company. As a visible figure in how people get paid, Cathy is often brought to the table when leaders are discussing how to better incentivize the attitudes and behaviors they want to observe on a daily basis, the kinds of behaviors that those leaders believe will align to eventual corporate growth.

Of course, it's more complicated than that.

Excerpts:

ME: What is the role that incentives have or do *not* in eliciting behaviors inside large companies? What are the successes or failures you've seen.

CATHY: Um, we only have an hour. [Laughs] Incentives are *not* just about annual bonus and pay. Along with pay, I think about the culture we are hoping to create and the performance we think we desire. Our thinking about compensation can only be considered as part of that overall culture, or else it is extremely easy to get mis-aligned.

ME: But I'd be surprised if leaders don't approach you with that very goal of "I want to change how my team goes to work."

Hasn't that been thrust at you as the Comp leader? Do you believe that's possible?

CATHY: Absolutely. The challenge is you're building a culture, not just a pay program. For example, I often get approached to create a compensation program to reward one team. I can do that! But if that team gets paid out and the company fails, is that okay? The one team gets paid, but nobody else. We have some portion of our leadership team to whom that is not okay. So some portion of my pay is to design programs that are relevant to individual employees but are also aligned to a culture we're trying to build.

ME: Are companies good or bad at moving the culture along with the incentive structure they want to bring forward?

CATHY: [Sigh] What I would say is this: Ultimately it is my goal to provide the knobs and levers that leaders need to differentiate the pay of high performers from low performers. I think that drives incentive and engagement. If somebody is a high performer, I want to make sure they understand this and feel differentiated, and I want to make sure you as a leader have the tools to do that.

ME: Okay …

CATHY: By the way, it might not be the bonus program! For you, for some reason, there could be other incentives that matter more.

■■■

ME: What innovations are you driving right now?

CATHY: We have some changes to the incentive programs we're trying to drive right now in the organization. And as part of that change, I'm utilizing some psychology. I'm introducing a change that I know will not be accepted. I'm purposely going farther than I want to in order to make our leaders uncomfortable …

ME: [Laughs] You're going full Limbaugh!

CATHY: Yeah. What I know is that, when I come back with something that's less aggressive, the leaders will say "Okay I think I can accept *that*."

■■

ME: What's the biggest change in your thinking over the last 5 years?

CATHY: It's that incentives go far beyond just cash pay. It's about opportunity. It's about making a difference. Work & Life balance. Your ability to innovate … and create something new. That all motivates people.

ME: I agree.

CATHY: The reality is that what's important to you is going to be specific to you, and different from most others. It's important to provide those levers to leaders to find and hit on those motivating factors.

ME: If you were going to rate leaders on their ability to do exactly that, from a scale of 1 being "Not at all" to 10 being "As good as I can imagine", what is the score of your median leader?

CATHY: I'd say a '4'. By the way, I would put myself as a 6. The reason is: It's hard. It's hard to have individualized conversations about why somebody's performance is different from another person's. And, then, there's noise. Even talking to your best employees and trying to explain why their performance last year was 'Outstanding' and this year is only 'Great' can be awkward, so most leaders just avoid it.

CHAPTER THREE: PEOPLE WITH THREE ARMS CAN'T BE TRUSTED

(Or, How you look to others, and why *you* are the strange one, not them)

In this last Chapter of Section One, we're going to focus on something you will truly hate: What people think about you! Alas - *you* will not seem normal to other people, and you need to understand that about yourself. In fact, you can often seem quite dangerous.

I break this down into three key categories: First of all, you're crazy. People will try to tell you continuously why your idea won't work. Second of all, you're scary. What you're saying is sometimes in direct conflict with ideals, principles or assumptions that have been safely in place (sometimes for decades). Finally, you're a threat. If what you're saying actually works, some of the people you're trying to work with may lose security of some sort – job, institutional knowledge, etc. They will not react lightly to this.

YOU'RE CRAZY

Here, I am talking about the idea that people will think you are legitimately unstable. Some of them will sit you down and, in careful tones clearly designed not to alarm you, will ask "What's wrong?" Or "Why are you doing this?" If you actually answer these questions honestly and inform them that you believe in your ideas or approach, they will then graduate to outright pity. You poor, stupid fool!, they will think.

Why is this? Well, companies don't get big in a day. It takes time, and over that time leaders are developed through the ranks and promoted up. Those leaders have 'seen things'. They know things. And some of those things will come out as "What you're suggesting has never worked. People have tried before. Heck, I've tried before."

To be clear – these people are not lying to you. They have seen people 'try it' before, and quite likely have tried what *you're* suggesting. But there are two important facets to this: By 'trying', they probably mean "I brought this up once in a committee, and it didn't get very far because I really hadn't thought it through completely." Second, none of those people who have tried it before are *you*. You are the differentiating factor. (Or, again, as I've said before, you may not actually be the differentiating factor but really, really wish you could be, which is why you are reading this book, all of which makes me kind of sad. But I'm going to continue on here as if you *are* one of these rare creatures who will leap ahead of the pack and be effective, because the rest of the book will get rather long if I have to continue caveating everything.)

Let me take each of these facets in turn. First, there is a very wide variation in people's vocabulary for the word 'try'. In my world, trying involves whipping up an actual funded project that even if it does not accomplish its goal, it does *prove* out that the idea did not work as theorized. Which, if you think about it, is its own success. For others, 'try' involves a lot of talk and an inability to get traction, therefore placing the idea in the scrap bin of history. I prefer my definition, and unless somebody can prove to you they've reached that ideal via their 'try', I would not be discouraged by their feedback and advice.

Second, and I want to be very clear here: Life is not fair or equitable. When somebody tells you something like "Look, I tried this before, nobody wants to do it that way", or "You'll never get funding for that project, I've tried a million times" they are relating their own (or others) inability to get things done. Of course, this may still be brilliant advice ... but it also may only reflect their personal experience. I have found big organizations to be in no way even playing fields, though – some people get funding for project just because of who they are, not because of what they're asking to do or how they asked to do it. Let me go so far as to say: Companies and leaders invest in people, not ideas. They fund projects because they like the ideas, but also often because they currently like (or are supporting) specific leaders, or perhaps they are just interested in funding the hobby of an up-and-coming executive who they would like to see step up and deliver some ROI on increasingly larger projects.

One last time – if you are SURE you're sitting on a great idea or project and can't get it started ... Maybe it's *just* you? Or, conversely, if you're the kind of person who's never had any trouble getting the backing & support for your ideas, however crazy, then I would say this – you need to understand this about yourself. The company and your leaders are *backing* you! You CAN get this done, even though the very attempt will seem unusual to people who haven't spent enough time around you to understand this about you.

YOU'RE SCARY

Let me pose a question to you, oh-great-changer-of-worlds: What if you're successful in your goals? What if you revolutionize your company? What will that mean to people around you? What does it signal about them? What does it imply about their knowledge, experiences & strategies?

If you answered, "It's probably not all that great for them", then you're on to something. And, potentially, you're talking out loud to yourself, so watch that – you're scary enough already.

Sports metaphors are lazy and obvious, but dammit so am I, so here goes: Let's think back to pro baseball over the last 20 years. There was a time where becoming the on-field Manager of a team seemed to have some specific requirements. First, you needed to be a former player. Second, you needed to understand certain things, like how you should put your fastest guys at the top of the order so they could steal bases and 'get into position to score'. Bunting was a valuable skill for moving players around the bases, so that tiny second baseman you kept on the roster still had some value. Batters who struck out too much were quick to find the bench. High batting averages were valuable – walks were not – so you got frustrated with guys who weren't up there hacking and you were delighted when they lifted a soft hit that dropped into short left field. Your center fielder played in center field, by which I mean 'straight out from home plate' – you might move him 20 steps this way or that, but not much more, and probably not until late innings. Your starting pitcher was your best pitcher, so you left him in the game until you absolutely *had* to pull him out.

Over the last 20 years, this has all radically changed. Statisticians have pointed out that you can't score if you don't get on base, so walks are as valuable as hits (or more so, since you're also forcing the opposing pitcher to waste more pitches on a non-out). Fielders are being moved all over the field – sometimes exposing entire sides of the field with zero or one defensive player – because so much is known about the tendencies of a particular batter. Pitchers are being removed from the game when they're throwing no-hitters, just because they've reached 90 total pitches thrown and, statistically, become less effective thereafter. Nobody steals a base, because unless you're successful more than 70% of the time, it's just not worth the risk of losing a precious base runner. And, by God, swing away – strike outs are just fine as long as you raise the chances of hitting a home run.

As this transition played itself out, the 'old school' did not understand. They pointed out flaws. They celebrated and championed the successes of those who did *not* yield to the new trends. But, ultimately … teams and Managers that did move quickly to these new approaches started to see out-sized returns.

All of this is a pretty good approximation of what you'll feel inside your large organization as you begin to bring your ideas – even well-articulated, meticulously supported ideas – to the forefront. To many leaders in the organization, you will simply be outright rejected since your ideas fly in the face of their own carefully developed concepts. And, remember – those ideas they're protecting did not come from *nowhere*. Those ideas were honed and developed over years, maybe decades, of results and success. Somehow the Kansas City Royals managed to win the 1985 World Series in spite of not knowing that stealing bases was a statistically invalid way of advancing your run scoring potential. So don't be surprised if the Manager of the 1985 Royals doesn't need or embrace your advice, thank you very much![11]

---

[11] I like to think there's at least one person out there reading that last comment thinking, "Crap! I *needed* Dick Howser on-board with this!"

Let's stick with that idea for a second, because it's important. Remember, in the metaphor above, you're not just introducing a new approach to stealing bases that you'll hope will be embraced and accepted. That would be the job of an Optimizer. No, you are suggesting that the very concept of stealing bases is useless and always has been. That is an attempt by you at invalidating the thinking of 100 years of leadership. You are telling them that they are wrong. And not just any 'them', you're telling *successful* people that they are wrong.

In an inherent and primal fashion, this will not feel right to people. How can we just be 'wrong'?, they will think. That flies in the face of the significant success those people have had. You must not have taken into consideration all of the nuance of this situation. You don't understand our customers, or our vendors, or our logistics process ... or much anything else, now that you've got 'them' started. Sure, your ideas sound good on paper, but in reality you will find they do not work. Because, if they did ... how could *we* have been so successful until now?

So, I'm about to pose another question, one I don't expect many leaders in this situation to actually ever think about ... But I expect their subconscious is churning on it while they're sitting across from you and your shmancy-pants new idea. And here it is: "What if you are right? What if there's a better way, one I'm not the expert on, one I didn't personally create? What if I'm not the right person for that new way of thinking? What if I'm not as important anymore?" These are questions that go beyond scary and start to pose the question of: "Are your ideas a threat?"

Artist's rendering of You in that Moment[vi]

FUCK YEAH, YOU'RE A THREAT

Things you might hear from a leader:

> *I have been leading payroll for the past ten years. We've had our ups-and-downs, and I can't believe we survived the PeopleSoft conversion three years ago, but we did. I'm well known for the fact that in those ten years we've never missed payroll – not once. Our tax returns get out on time, too, which the leaders of my organization appreciate.*
>
> *And, now, here you are with your ideas for outsourcing payroll. I'm not immediately a fan of this plan.*
>
> *First, of course, outsourcing is more expensive. You pay a premium – everybody knows that. And, you lose*

flexibility by having to commoditize the payroll process: ABC Company has been putting out payroll every week for the last 10 years, and by going to ACME Payroll we have to covert to paying every *two* weeks instead. Oh, and what about that time during the Cleveland power blackout when we found a way to airlift the pay checks into the city for all our employees there? You think ACME's going to do that? I sure don't.

Plus, I've been telling you all about this great new Paycard system I've been working with our vendors to set-up. That's really going to speed things up and cut costs. I'd like to see us play that out before we make any drastic decisions about outsourcing. I think it will really change your minds about the value of a great internal payroll team!

Things I doubt that same leader will say out loud:

Didn't I bring this idea of outsourcing up about 8 years ago? All of you didn't like it then, why do you like it now?

That Peoplesoft conversion was hard. I mean, REALLY hard. My team is pretty mature and does not take change well – it was literally torture getting them to learn the new system. And I know we need to do *another* upgrade pretty soon if we're going to stay supported by our software vendor. I'd love to avoid that somehow, and I know outsourcing gives me some of that flexibility since it would become the outsourcer's problem to stay current on technology.

Of course, I don't actually know the first thing about running an outsource-heavy shared services team.

What if I'm not good at that? Who's going to replace me? Is it *you*? Are you just doing this to get my job?

It's important to remember that you and your idea did not appear in a vacuum. That team / division / company had a 'before you arrived' and some semblance of a plan for 'later'. There have been high's and low's. There were strategies that were glorious successes and a few bombs along the way. Each of these people has allies shaped by battles young-and-old.

As you begin your innovative ways, you and your project are a threat. A threat to jobs, to high-paying salaries, to careers that are *this* close to retirement, to careers that just got started, to ideas that haven't been seen all the way out, to focus that was so recently gained and to wins that will be (because of you) quickly forgotten.

This is serious shit. Somewhere in the pack are a few (or many) people who are impacted exactly as described above, and they will subconsciously resist your changes and ideas. You must have a plan for how you, my reader and leader, will deal with this reality. I will repeat it again-and-again: A good idea is not enough.

Let me share an old blog post I wrote that emphasizes this point:

A BETTER TOMORROW IS <u>NOT</u> ENOUGH

An argument broke out near me recently regarding TSA security enhancements at airports, and whether the intrusive protocols were acceptable in exchange for increased safety. It made me think: my real problem with air travel isn't the security, it's the long wait to get through security (and the anxiety I feel about how early I have to arrive at the airport). I ended up wondering how much of the outrage has *to do with the TSA procedures themselves versus the fact these security requirements are simply being layered on top of our pre-existing problems with an already broken process. Said another way – if the new TSA procedures *reduced* your time in queue from 45 minutes to 5 minutes, but still required the same physical intrusiveness, I wonder if a more positive response would have been received.*

To the same end, which of the following would you find acceptable?:

- In exchange for another 10 minutes in the airport security line applying a special sticker to each piece of luggage, the airport <u>guarantees</u> that your risk of losing your luggage will be significantly reduced (though, obviously, not eliminated completely).

- A new transparent spray-on material has been developed for your car that will guarantee, if you *do* get into an accident, that your vehicle will not be damaged in any way. Unfortunately, it needs to be manually sprayed on before each commute, which adds another 15 minutes each way.

- The new tax code requires every tax payer to spend 30 minutes getting their annual federal taxes reviewed by an official auditor. However, because fraud will decrease, tax rates will stabilize at today's rates instead of growing each year, as otherwise has been predicted.

I'm guessing none of these ideas are particularly exciting to you. What's interesting to me is that while the outcome is appealing (Improved safety! Less lost baggage! Stable taxes!), those outcomes are achieved by piling more bad news on top of a process you already deeply dislike (Longer commutes! More time thinking about your taxes! More time in line!). And, in cases like these, people simple cannot be rational and do the math over whether the investment outweighs the benefits.

But, *should* they? In today's world people have come to expect that progress of any sort has direct benefits and indirect benefits. "Inventing something that reduces the risk of lost baggage? Great! It should probably do something about the long lines, too. Wait, it does the exact opposite and lengthens that line instead? Then it's completely unacceptable. I am not willing to invest now for returns later."

My point (and I do have one, I think): you are attempting to drive a lot of change *and* a lot of value via your efforts. When you make these changes, you expect people to go about the effort of getting trained, or dealing with temporary slow-downs during the learning curve, or to advocate for these changes within their leadership group.

But beware – if what you hope to achieve during all of this steps on any pre-existing and sensitive organizational nerves, it may not matter *what* benefits you're offering farther down the road.

Best case: your hot new idea/widget solves not only the downstream problem, but also offers some relief to the proverbial long line at the front of the airport.

YOU'RE THE STRANGE ONE, NOT THEM

The easiest, most repetitive and most cliched conversation I've had in the business world is about how much our co-workers suck. You can kick off a conversation with anybody with these simple words: "Can you believe [INSERT NAME OF CO-WORKER HERE]? That guy/lady! He/She really doesn't get it.[12]" Almost anybody will join in on this conversation. (By the way, for those that don't take that bait, you can rest assured that they are having the same conversation somewhere else about *you*.)

But, why? Why is this something that all people do? Are we all just bat-shit crazy and can't help but rail on each other in this ultra-competitive rat race of a life we all chose to lead?

Yes. Yes, we are. But there's more to the story, and the better you understand it, the more you can work the system to accomplish your goals.

---

[12] It's so cliched, you can just say those literal words above. "Have you met NAME OF CO-WORKER? Can you believe him/her?" Nobody will notice, they're so eager to start railing on their co-workers.

NO SOCIOPATHS

Okay, I've established we're all crazy. But, I want to be clear – that's just humanity. We love to gossip, we love to complain. Every time we talk shit about a co-worker we elevate ourselves, at least in our own minds. It feels good, and it's hard to stop. I'm not surprised by it.

In fact, that's sort of my point – when I see people behaving like humans, I don't get surprised. We are humans! (Again, this is the sort of top-notch observation you parted your hard-earned money to get). In fact, I've made a great living in my career *expecting* people to behave like humans.

In over 25 years of working in large companies, I still to this day do not believe I have ever worked with a sociopath (defined as somebody whose behavior is so random and wicked it seems to lack any sort of normal human conscience). Rather, I believe that every single person I've worked with has behaved rationally and according to the incentives provided to them. Sometimes those incentives are not obvious, but they exist, and the more I probe to understand them the more I can learn to anticipate and guide the actions of my co-workers.

Understand the incentives, understand the person.

WE BEHAVE RATIONALLY

Now, I'm not going to tell you that I haven't worked with some terrible people. Oh, I have. And, yet, I would *still* define these people as uber-rational. They understand and covet their incentives so strongly that it produces outsized actions on their part … actions that many people found objectionable and perhaps even worked against the desired goals of the company or team as a whole. But that didn't make these people irrational. Hell, no.

Let me share a story. In one of my roles, I worked with the President of a large national retailer. One day he complained to me about how his team was regularly outspending its payroll budget at the store level. He explained that he had *dramatically* increased the points assigned to 'making payroll' on each store leader's bonus plans. He couldn't understand why those same store leaders would throw away bonus dollars by routinely scheduling above the payroll guidelines they were provided. To him, this seemed like a set of actions that were against the incentives these people were provided.

I saw it differently. To bring him along, I asked him about the surprise non-announced visits he made to these stores throughout the year. First, I asked him if he was provided visit guides for each store ahead of time that told him whether the store was making payroll ("No", he admitted). Second, I asked him what he focused on during those visits, to which he told me that his primary focus was on well-organized back rooms and clean, good-looking store for the shoppers. I reminded him that those outcomes could be achieved ahead of one of his visits, even in poorly run stores, by over-spending payroll guidelines. Finally, I asked him what the worst-case scenario was to the store leaders (and district supervisors) when he made on of his store visits. He told me that it was not unusual for him to fire store leaders on-the-spot if he was unhappy with what he saw.

So, based on his responses, I did some math for him. Basically, to my eyes, his store leaders were following his incentives *extremely* well. They were mentally balancing the loss of bonus they would receive, a bad result they would have to deal with 1 day per year when their disappointing bonuses were paid, against the 365-day threat of losing their income altogether and without much warning.   If a store leader was making $125k per year with the potential of a $75k bonus, the upside of $200k was actually *less* on their minds than the downside of making $0k per year.   Therein lied the results.

How did we adjust?   We changed the visit guides to show payroll spending versus budget for the last few months.   If the payroll results were not favorable, the visit to the store ended at the front door with the store manager getting chewed out (and, potentially, put on warning if this was ongoing, documented behavior).   Word got around quickly and, within months, a substantially smaller percentage of store managers were overspending their payroll budgets.   Incentives changed, and so did behaviors.

People are rational.   Understand the incentives, understand the behavior (and learn what to do next).

PEEL THE ONION AND FIND THE INCENTIVES

A concept like 'Understand the Incentives' is not as simple as it might first appear.   People aren't simple, but I find that most attempts to understand incentives stop at surface level by considering pay.   And, yes, pay is a very big factor in what drives workers.

But, *you* as an innovator are going to be involved in a lot of projects that impact teams and leaders in different ways than their pay.   You need to recognize and understand all of these incentives and be able to react to them.   These incentives include: Money, Power, Stress, Priority and Glory.

INCENTIVE #1 - MONEY: First of all, money is an obvious incentive and when I use the word 'incentives' that's what most people assume I'm talking about. In fact, they can't see *past* the idea of money = incentives and incentives = money.

For example, if my personal bonus paid a significant amount (let's say, 20% of my salary) for how much time I spent in the lobby of my office building, that's where I'd hold all my meetings, professional lunches and team events. I would be a fixture of that lobby space. "Brian spends a *lot* of time in the lobby," people would be heard to say, and they would be correct. It probably wouldn't make any sense to the rest of you, as my personal bonus structure is not as public or apparent as you might presume. To most of you, I would look eccentric. But it would still be *rational* behavior on my part, even if *you* don't fully understand what I'm doing, or why.

There was an event I once experienced where a group had come up with an idea that would save their company $100 million in expenses. I'm not kidding - $100 million American, which (if enacted) would go straight to the bottom-line. Good God. Of course, if I'm bringing this story up, it must be true that the leadership team said "no" to this idea, and that's exactly what happened. We were flabbergasted (our flabbers were entirely gasted, I tell you!). The idea laid dead for 6 months. Finally, I had a conversation with the merchant team and they asked me, "Why do we care about expense savings? I get paid on sales growth and margin rate, and this project doesn't help either." Bingo.

Three weeks later – enough time for a few meetings with compensation – and that merchant team was *entirely* on-board with the expense savings initiative. Couldn't have been more excited! So, again – money can be a tremendous driver of incentives and decision-making, but that money is not always pointed in the *direction* you might think.

In fact, let me go a step farther – money is almost ALWAYS not pointed in the best interests of the company. Now, I'm not suggesting that employees act against the companies that employ them. No, no. No. Well … okay, yes, I guess that's what I'm suggesting. I'm just saying it's nothing evil, just human nature[13]. It's very, very difficult to design pay & incentive programs that fully align an organization toward one objective. Your job, as the innovator in this company, is to understand this, anticipate it and peel the onion to understand what conflicts may exist. You may even need to correct those conflicts in order to move forward with your plans.

But, as I said earlier, money isn't even close to being the only definition of the word 'incentives'. Power can be another motivator. Sometimes you'll run into people who will reject your ideas for the simple reasons that 1) they did not come up with those ideas, and 2) your very existence and ideas are a threat to the control they exert over the organization (or, at least, their silo of that organization).

INCENTIVE #2- POWER: This tends to be most true with very tenured leaders, people who have been in control of their function for a decade or more. These are people who are often in the most need of innovative ideas and progress, but they do not see it that way. In their eyes, people like you have come-and-gone, and those people's stupid ideas have fucked up this-and-that and it took X years to recover from that effort, or whatever. I'm not saying they're wrong about what happened in the past, but as I've said before – what happened in the past is never a good indication of what's going to happen in the future when it comes to innovation,

---

[13] By now you're noticing that I keep coming back to those words a lot. 'Human nature'. It's important, and most of you are *terrible* at recognizing it, whether you understand that or not. So there. Write your own book if you don't like it.

as the key factor to success in these spaces is the leader of those projects (which, in our case, is *you*). But they don't know that, and they are going to resist.

So, what is the motivation of these leaders? First, you have to understand their current situation. Often, within their space, they are kings and lord-makers. People faithful to the king have been incredibly rewarded over the years, rising fast. These 'lords of the land' have learned how to get things done with the king and are often the kind of people who you hear say, "I know how to talk to him". The king's entire organization maintains strict command-and-control layers – you are *not* to approach the king without first speaking to the lords. This further elevates and empowers these lords in ways they, too, will ultimately want to protect, while making the king-figure seem even more imposing and powerful from afar.

Good God that's complicated, right? Just ... why? The most obvious answer is that 'Power is fun' and so is having the reverence and fear of others, which might be occasionally true but is not something that I usually believe. Rather, those leaders' answers would probably sound more like, "I have learned how to get things done in this organization and have carefully crafted my team to make it so we're able to do exactly that."

In many cases, these long-tenured leaders were part of founding and launching their business lines. They are walking history books of the effort, wins, losses and outright debacles that went along with getting their space off-the-ground. If there's anything you should be taking away from this book, it's this – IT IS NOT EASY to get nascent business lines or processes running inside big organizations. Frankly, it's no easier than being an innovator. These leaders *should* be admired for what they've accomplished. But the same skills that allowed them to be successful in growing their business can (and often do) become a detriment over time. They do not see it that way, but it is true.

In working with these leaders, your approach must consider the extent to which these leaders will go to maintain the careful control (read: Power) they have over their organization. In fact, they will resist even the simplest changes from the larger corporation, much less you. Even something as innocuous as changes to how PTO days are managed for employees become high-drama situations with these leaders.

So, if they are going to be pains for the people making *small* changes to the organization, how do you think they will respond to you, a legitimate threat coming into *their* space? Therefore, your approach must consider their power and either cater to it (ie, make them more powerful) or permanently reduce it.

Read that last sentence again – those are the options. Ouch. In this situation it will *always* be a power struggle, because the kings will make it into one even if you don't. For those of you reading this who are truly up to this type of challenge, you'd better be thinking something along the lines of: "Before I even say 'Yes' to being involved in this project, I had better understand the situation I'm facing and align myself with the highest leaders of the company to back me up on what needs to be done. Those C-suite executives had better understand the situation, even if I have to have very frank conversations with them about what may be necessary to be successful. If those C-suite leaders hedge on this reality *at all*, I should turn down this project graciously, but immediately."

Remember - it is not about *winning*, though it will feel that way some days. Resist that feeling. Your job is not to 'win' some kind of power struggle. It is about moving forward and doing what it takes to get the job done.

INCENTIVE #3 – STRESS: You have a refined and powerful idea. You have the presentation nailed. Your pitch is good. It's the right idea at the right time for the company. It's affordable. It's doable. And, yet, you get a "no" from leadership.

What *you* don't know can be extensive – perhaps, in this case, this leader is fighting for their job. They've had three consecutive quarters of sales misses. The CEO has been all-too-clear that his patience is waning. Their team is starting to question their direction. And, just to top it off, their daughter is about to head off to China for two semesters abroad studying *philosophy*, of all the damn things.

How do you find out if stress is a factor in your inability to move projects forward with that leader? On this one, you're probably going to have to ask around. Your network, if properly broad, should know. Make sure you're tapping into them before-and-after your meeting with the leader. Find out what you can about the *situation*, not just the potential appeal of your project.

In these circumstances where stress *is* an identifiable factor, you'd better figure out how your project *reduces* that stress. You need to address this directly and clearly, identifying (as part of your pitch) what problems the leader has, why your project directly reduces or eliminates those problems, the odds of success and the timeline. Pitching your idea in this framework shows your are empathetic and in-tune with the situation, without outright saying "Let's save your ass, here."

INCENTIVE #4 – PRIORITY: You have no idea how many balls these leaders are juggling. It's a lot. There comes a time when leaders must limit their exposure to new ideas, even really good ideas … and this is a *good* thing.

There are two clear categories of prioritization:

1) Too much to do – at a certain point, a leader has to face that quarter-end is coming, that they're down two critical headcount, that they've just had a poor sales month, that their in-stocks are not meeting expectations, that they're on two external Boards of Directors, and on-and-on. Now, here comes *you* with your good (or maybe even great) idea and all of this energy. Frankly, they can't even, and so you get a 'no'.

Note that this may be a "no for now", which is a situation where you should follow up on in six months to see if things have changed. How do you find this out? Well, first – you don't go charging into the situation with your head full of steam and vomiting 'ideas' all over the leader's office. Instead, make sure your conversation with that leader has a point built into it pretty early on where you ask about their goals for the current year. What is their team working on? What's their most important problem? It's a great chance to understand where their heads are really at before you come at them too strongly. It allows you to place your idea within their framework and construct of goals, if possible.

One other thing to note about this example – some bosses are really clever and don't actually tell you "no". These leaders aren't very common, but when I run into them I'm always impressed. They're the kind of people who will listen to your idea, let you know (with true clarity) that they don't have any resources to devote to the project, but instead of rejecting you they encourage you. They ask for more analysis. They ask for your leadership and for you to seek out additional sponsors. In their minds, they think: "Heck, I *would* like the outcome this person is selling, and while I can't devote any time to it ... maybe if I encourage them they'll do it on their own!" Don't let yourself get suckered into these situations – you need their direct sponsorship. Otherwise, as I said above ... let the idea simmer for 6 months and come back and try again. Timing is everything.

2) Alignment – Some ideas, no matter how good, just aren't important to the goals of the organization. I'm reminded of a famous example involving Southwest Airlines, whose motto (for years) was to be "*the* low cost airline". They lived that principle. According to the story[14], an ambitious executive approached the CEO about adding a new variety of salads as a meal choice for passengers. These particular salads were very trendy and could benefit the image of the airline while generating some in-flight revenue. The CEO thanked the executive for the idea and then asked how the salads would help Southwest Airlines deliver on its promise of being *the* low-cost airline. Obviously, there was no correct answer, and the idea was shelved.

Sometimes it's just a great idea in the wrong place, which is a failure of neither the idea-generator nor the business. In fact, the best part about this Southwest Airlines example is that they had a *guiding principle* by which to make the decision of whether or not to pursue the (presumably good) idea. When they said no, everybody knew why! Many, many companies do not have this.

I worked for an organization that suffered from this. If an idea emerged that could generate profits, it was pursued. The company treated each Board of Directors meeting with the same sense of

---

[14] Potentially apocryphal.

urgency (or more) than they gave to their highest-cost IT project or their latest acquisition. In other words, prioritization was completely lacking. This stretched their resources, created unnecessary conflicts and pretty much guaranteed that the best possible outcome of any effort was 50% of what was desired. As the adage goes, 'When everything is a priority, nothing is'. So, bottom-line: When somebody tells you that your idea doesn't fit the priorities of the organization, that's a really good thing to stop and think about. *Maybe* they're wrong, but maybe, just maybe, they're right and you're the one learning an important lesson.

INCENTIVE #5 – GLORY: I'm just going to be honest here – this is probably the least common and least useful incentive. The reality is that, for most of the leaders you will need to influence, they have already achieved *plenty* of glory. It's right in the VP / EVP titles they get to carry. They don't need much more, and frankly they're wise enough to understand that the pursuit of glory simply doesn't pay off in many cases, at least not in the way they might hope. These are not stupid people, or naïve.

However, there are circumstances when Glory matters. For example, a major corporation I once worked with decided to expand its operations internationally. For the leadership team that was tapped to deliver the international results, it was all-systems go. The chance to prove themselves as C-suite level leaders was irresistible. Even when unrealistic expectations were put on the timeline for this international expansion, the C-suite team exuded nothing but confidence. These leaders wanted The Prize!

The point here is that in the right circumstances, leadership can be influenced and incentivized to make moves that might, otherwise, go outside their own core needs if they see significant glory in it for themselves. These people have to be motivated by reputation and long-term thinking, especially on a personal level.

'Ambitious' would not be sufficient a word for describing these people.

The downside - *you* often do not have the power necessary to influence these people. It's Board-level or C-suite level 'gifts' that must be made available in order to package these sort of opportunities. If you happen to be the sort of person who has influence at those levels within your organization – a mentor on the Board (particularly in the compensation committee) or an old boss who's made it to the C-suite and still looks to you for innovation – perhaps you can help to develop and influence these packages. But, for most of you, probably not.

These are just examples of incentives that go into motivating leaders to make decisions or take chances that you want them to take. This section of the book is deliberately expansive to give you the idea of how much work *must* go into understanding incentives in order for you to be successful as an innovator. Many (if not most) of you will fail simply because of your inability to truly understand why people behave like they do.

RISK-TAKING IS PROBABLY GENETIC

It gets worse.

You are not a risk taker. In writing this, I am relatively confident that I'm accurate for 95% of the people reading this text. Even people that I would classify as 'innovators' for the purposes of writing this book tend not to be true risk takers.

Who is a risk taker? Let's look at exaggerated examples. Richard Branson is one that pops to mind. Here's a person who could decide tomorrow that the key to developing a fleet of self-driving cars is to permanently suspend a thousand GPS-enabled hot-air balloons over North America and to build an army of squirrels with laser beams attached to their tails. Parts of this idea wouldn't make sense to me, and maybe not to you, either ... but the thing about Mr. Branson is that he goes all-in on his ideas, pushes people well beyond the point where others would give up on those ideas as impossible and is willing to be *spectacularly* wrong. He does pull out of some ideas and shut them down, but his reasons for shutting things down are very different than yours or mine would be.[15] Risk means something very different for him. It means the idea was attempted and failed-as-designed, not that somebody believed it would never work from the beginning.

Do you know your risk tolerance? This is important. Why? Because in some cases you will run into people along your mission of innovation whose risk tolerance is very, very different from your own. You will meet some people who are so risk-averse (maybe even waaay more than you) they will try to stop your efforts anyway that they can. They will talk about you as irresponsible. There are others who are naturally more Branson-like who want to see if they can pull off whatever crazy idea you're nurturing. These people can be valuable, but you have to understand their perspective and tendencies as you consider what you're trying to pull off.

The point is – you had better understand what your risk tolerance is and the same for the key partners (and stakeholders) you're taking on whatever journey you have planned. For low-risk tolerance stakeholders, they are going to need a lot of venting time with you and explanations on what's happened, and why. Tell them, up front, that you want more time with them than would otherwise seem natural. Make sure you're sharing the story of your project with them – don't leave it to them to "fill in the blanks" for

---

[15] My own would probably be something like: "I have reached my limit for spending on laser-equipped squirrels."

themselves, or you'll be fighting reputational issues throughout your project. For high-risk stakeholders, make sure there is a voice of reason present to balance their thinking. I don't mean to mute them – you should just have somebody around who asks good questions when they get over-enthusiastic about what's possible. You are not Richard Branson and don't have his vast fortune to fall back on in case of significant failure. The company will have to account for your failure(s) in their quarterly earnings calls, and you'll never want to put the CEO in a position to have to use the words "squirrel lasers" as an explanation for shortfalls.

TAKE-AWAYS

And that's it for Section One! These first three chapters have been about introducing the concepts, ideas and forces that make Innovation such a difficult activity inside large companies. Understanding these forces is *crucial* to your ability to build a plan to deal with them as you start to construct your project.

And now, in Section Two, we'll pivot to exactly that – constructing an approach to achieving *your* goals.

Let's see how that goes!

SECTION TWO: HOW DO YOU *DO* IT?

In this section of the book, I move from the construct of 'innovation' to the practical advice *you'll* need to ~~salvage the remnants of your career~~ be successful in your projects!

We'll cover:

1) What specific problems you're going to be facing as you strike out on your project
2) The tools you need
3) Important actions for you to take
4) Issues that come up during *any* project

CHAPTER FOUR: A timeline of unavoidable crap

(Or: What you're going to be facing as you start implementing innovative approaches)

So, you got your wish and your innovative project, which is chock-full of innovation, was approved by the suddenly innovative leadership team because of your innovative approach to getting them to be innovative. Swell! You're an innovator!

Yeah! Woo! Uh ... oh, you're really doing this, huh?

I mean, it's great that you did all that work and got a project going. That is *not* easy. It's just that you're not even close to done filling the role of an innovator. Rather, you're now unfortunately a target for all sorts of problems that come with the job.

This chapter is dedicated to understanding the factors and forces you will face now that you're underway. Understanding these things helps you anticipate them and prepare for them *in your project plan*. Do not deal with these things as they come up – expect them, talk about them with your team and prepare yourselves with action plans.

We'll talk more about building out those Project Plans in Chapter Six, but for now we're introducing the elements you need to prepare to face.

BAD TIMING

Quit. Just quit. At least for a while. Maybe completely.

It's advice I've given on multiple occasions. I'm sitting with a peer, a partner, or a mentee, who's describing the issues they're having pushing through a project. "It's the exact right idea! We've got management support!", they tell me. "Why can't the rest of the people see the changes we need to make?"

Because they can't. They're not 'wrong' or 'flawed', they're just human (*inexcusably* so, but nevertheless). But, here's the good news – *you're* not necessarily wrong either. Your idea might just be the thing that will help your company grow, expand or become more profitable. But, it could just be the wrong time.

Here's the problem – your idea does not exist in a vacuum. Let's say that you've just handed your brilliant idea, the 'Pet Rock, but more Pettier'[16], across the desk to the company's product manager. Its brilliance is undeniable. You've even sold it well. But, to your shock, the answer is "no" – maybe even a polite no, but still no. Why? Is this person an idiot?

Yes, of course they are (honestly, I don't know how you make it through the day). But that's not the point. The point is that this moron also has a life outside of this meeting with you. He may already have three products in development he's promised the CEO will be released within the current quarter, and he can't afford any current distractions from this goal. Or, he's in the middle of re-organizing his team, a full-time effort. Or, he's been ordered to reduce his budget by 20% to help offset a recent product failure. There are any number of reasons that a person might stare at the very best idea and pass.

---

[16] Mine! That's mine now.

The big lesson I'd want you to take away from this is (and you're not going to like it): Good ideas are actually a dime-a-dozen. If leadership was simply about rejecting the *bad* ideas that came across your desk, more people would be good leaders … and we both know that simply isn't true. The reality is that (most) bad ideas do get shown the dust bin. The problem is that leaders are shown many good ideas over the course of a year and it is the sorting through those good ideas to choose which ones you're actually going to pursue that helps amazing leaders stand out from average ones. Like it or not, leaders are *paid* to ignore (some) really good ideas in order to prioritize the best ideas.

So, does that mean you should give up? Absolutely not! If your idea is truly worthwhile, if it is truly a differentiated concept, then it will have its day. It will come back! Times change with the tide, and you'll be surprised how that idea will boomerang back in three months, or six, or a year. Suddenly it will be important. Suddenly it will have legs. And, just as suddenly, this idea you've been begging to get started will be considered *behind in your timeline* because all the eyes will be on you to deliver. But, have faith – good ideas do win out.

If your idea doesn't have legs and doesn't come back around to getting attention, then it probably wasn't that good to begin with. Suck it up – it happens to the best of us.

THE BUREAUCRACY

So, you've made it through whatever your company's process is for capital allocation and got your project and its funding approved. Congratulations! Prepare to enter a state of disillusionment that only large companies and the government can bring: Powerful, unrelenting 'rules' that will contradict all sense of common-sense, as well as the people who *love* those rules and will test your sanity with them.

For example, if your project is like most you will have asked for some headcount as part of your pitch for funding. You will have been very clear that you need 4-5 new people, and you will have stressed these people do *not* exist today at the company. You will have carefully emphasized that without these people, your project will fail. You went through all of the careful scrutiny from the C-Suite that goes along with such a request – after all, they don't just give away headcount. During those project reviews you will have carefully checked with those leaders to ensure you were interpreting their signals correctly, specifically how they were nodding their agreement and giving their outright consent for you to move forward. This consent includes (and here was where you were particularly careful) the hiring of the new headcount you require. You will walk toward the door exiting the capital allocation committee meeting believing that, *if any one thing is true in the entire universe in that moment*, you have been given the right to hire those 4-5 people.

You silly, stupid fool.

Instead, prepare for some meetings. For example, when you attempt to post the new positions you need, the Finance and HR teams may sit you down to explain the company is currently under a headcount freeze, and that to get the headcount you need you'll have to ask first if any of the *other* department heads will agree to give up the 4-5 positions you'll need from their budget (which, of course, is hilarious). Or, they'll suggest – even the people who were in the room with you at the time you made the request and listened to you carefully emphasize that the talent you needed to do the project could *not* be found internally – that you should first try to re-assign internal staff to fill the roles.

Also, there is nowhere in the building for your people to sit. HQ is full, sorry. And remote working is not allowed.

There will also be problems getting the signed sheets down to IT so they can get a new project set up in their project management systems, which is required before they can sign an official Project Manager to your work. This will take weeks if you don't hound them.

HR will want to know what expense center the new people will be charged to – yes, the ones they won't approve you to hire – and they will need information from you that (take a deep breath here) only HR could *possibly* know, attributes that exist only within their people management systems but are not available or shared with anybody outside of HR. You will tell them that there is no way you could know this, and that shouldn't *they* have this information, and they will explain that *you* should get this HR information from Finance, which will make you ask them why they didn't just call Finance in the first place.

Also, now that your project is approved, people in Procurement may get frustrated because if you *really* wanted the servers / tools / equipment / whatever that was listed in your project funding request, you really should have been ordering that stuff months ago because there is a significant lead time to getting it. You will remind them that *they* were involved in helping you estimate the costs of that stuff when you put together your capital request, so why didn't they mention this before today? But they will explain that there's a big difference between estimating for stuff and the work you should have been doing to prepare for actually ordering it. So, that's on you, pal.

Procurement will let you know that they've run out of laptops. Can your new team wait until there's enough turnover elsewhere in the organization to free up some computers? Also, before you can get those laptops, they're going to need to know which cubes your team will be sitting in. No cube numbers, no computers.

Finance will send you a note asking you to forecast the spending of your project by week, including estimates of what part of that spending can be 'capitalized'. You will carefully explain that such estimates are currently impossible, given that you've barely started the project so any spending outside of the next few weeks would be incredibly difficult to guess. They will listen to you carefully, and then ask if you received the forecasting template they just sent you by e-mail. They're due Tuesday.

I'm only grazing the surface with these stories, unfortunately. Bottom-line: There can be nothing more depressing as a leader than the weeks immediately following getting approval for your project. A time you might otherwise think would be a whirlwind of progress toward your 'dream ambition' will instead be a test of your organization, perseverance and patience. However, this is a moment when your team is truly depending on you to break down walls and keep things moving. You can't get disillusioned now.[17]

There is another acute danger: You can fall *really* far behind your timeline during this phase if you don't doggedly follow-up on every to-do, every "you need to talk to [Person X]" and, every reminder to HR that your jobs still needs to be posted, etc. You must have strong project management skills to get yourself to the point where a team is assembled, where problems have been sufficiently understood and mitigated and where there is movement forward on your actual project.

---

[17] There will be much better times for disillusionment later. Also, while we're talking: Can one get 'illusioned'? Or is it just 'disillusioned'? Feel free to discuss.

THE INEVITABLE: SOMETHING WILL GO WRONG

Being a 'project manager' for truly innovative initiatives is a bit of a misnomer. Yes, you must be on top of things and have a system by which you will monitor progress and keep track of the multiple 'tracks' that will be going on at the same time – personnel, IT management, budget oversight, communication, etc. However, you will not be able to anticipate the various challenges, compromises and adaptations you'll make as the project progresses. This is not to say the project will go badly or that you won't be able to achieve your goals; rather, I'm trying to emphasize that the 'unknowns' embedded in innovation projects will make any detailed long-term planning that you might attempt almost immediately obsolete. The noted auteur Mike Tyson coined the phrase[18]: "Everybody has a plan until the first time they get punched in the face."

This practicality will bother many people. Leaders will want to understand your A-to-Z plan. They will want to see and review that documentation. And you will have such a plan[19] – effective project management is critical. It's just that the plan is going to change, especially those elements that are farther out in your timeline. If you make it to Point 'G' on your A-to-Z plan without having something go wrong, consider yourself lucky.

So, instead of Project Manager, I suggest a term more like Project Owner. The buck stops here.

So, how do you own a plan and effectively lead a team when even *you* don't know 1) what's going to go wrong, and 2) what's going to change when it does? You can't! Good night, everyone! Don't forget to tip your waiters.

---

[18] At least as far as I know, he did.
[19] We'll get into project planning templates in Chapter 6.

That said, here are some things that will be important to your success:

1) Don't panic – good leaders understand that any reaction they exhibit, be it panic, anger or random reactions, will be amplified ten-fold as it trickles down through their team and organization. If you panic at a scale of 3 of 10, you can bet your team leaders are making that a 6 of 10 by the time they talk to their teams, and the team members themselves will go straight to 10. Under no circumstances will this help. *Expect* things to go wrong and be cool when it does.

2) Act the part – you are leading a project, initiative or turnaround that is inherently risky. If you over-react when things go wrong, you're revealing yourself as a rookie … and, perhaps, the kind of person who should not be leading this type of project. When somebody tells you bad news, your behavior should project that you *understood* bad news was inevitable and begin the mitigation actions you have prepared for just such a situation[20]. Anything else – especially anger – will ultimately just cause questions about your leadership. Worse, it could keep people from telling you when the next thing goes wrong.

3) Have a great team, especially leaders – when something goes wrong, you need to understand it. You need input from people you can trust, and those people had better be the leaders you've surrounded yourself with on this project. You should be able to turn to your HR, IT, Finance, Operations, Legal and other partners, and those people should be qualified to tell you what the issue is and what

---

[20] You have those, right? I meant to mention that before. My bad.

the options are based on their experienced perspectives. This leadership team will be tested throughout your efforts – choose wisely.[21]

4) Have a process for effective debate – Even when things are going well, you should have routine meetings with your leadership team to review the status of your projects. Everybody should attend every meeting – don't start your meetings unless everybody shows up, and make sure that's the expectation. Everybody should be speaking and providing their thoughts. Make sure debate is encouraged (you'll have to lead this – if you ever get consensus too quickly, search for somebody to provide the devil's advocate position).

If you've followed this approach, then when things *do* go wrong, it won't seem unnatural when you assemble the team and ask for their thoughts and opinions. It will be like any other meeting. This will provide a sense of calmness to the proceedings that you need when important decisions – decisions that everybody may not agree with – need to be made.

5) Don't expect consensus – when things go wrong, they will probably not go wrong in ways that are easy to mitigate. If your issues can be solved with a simple 10-minute conversation and everybody agrees on the same path forward, you probably have not had a real problem. So, when your leaders (inevitably) don't agree on how to solve a serious problem, you don't want and can't expect them to

---

[21] Chapter 5 will get into exactly how to set-up and run these leadership/partner meetings.

all just agree on one path forward. Listen to everybody, make sure you repeat back the various sides and risks you've heard from each of them ... and then *you* will have to make a decision that will leave at least some of them upset. You're the Project Owner - that's the way it is.

6) Have a process for change management and communication to team and stakeholders – once decisions have been made on a new path forward, you must communicate-communicate-communicate that change. Leaders, Executives, team members, key stakeholders and others must *all* know and understand the change that has happened and what you weighed in making that decision. You need a way to test if this information is getting out to everybody – ask questions in meetings, send out surveys ... do something that asks the question: "Do you know what we're doing *now* that things have changed?"

7) Have a process for vetting that the project plan is updated after the new path forward has been declared. Individual silos of your project will need to make the adjustments to their plans – personnel, IT management, budget overview, etc. – and then a *public* meeting should be held with all players to review the changes. People should discuss the adjustments they made to their segments, showing how expectations & dates have moved. There *should* be reactions from the other segments as these revisions are made public for the first time. For example, if the timing for hiring of key personnel is changing, the HR team will probably get reactions from the IT team (who might depend on those resources) and budget team (who might have guessed wrong about how & when the new team would

start). Adjustments will need to be made, and it should all be done in public to avoid the chances of certain groups not being informed. Assume nothing.

THE BLAME: IT WON'T MATTER THAT YOU TOLD PEOPLE ABOUT 'IT', THEY'LL STILL BE UPSET

If you've been doing your job well, you've spent a great deal of time communicating with key stakeholders at various points of your initiative. Those communication points may have happened during the initial funding phases, or in follow-up status checks, or during steering committee meetings, or via e-mail, or more. The point is, you should have been sharing *constantly*.

So, when things go wrong, you'll be able to lean on that effort as you attempt to keep executives and key stakeholders calm, right?

STUPID HUMAN! Of course not.

About half of the people you talk to will react like they had *no idea* this kind of problem/issue/error/risk/screw-up could happen, and it will be clear from their tone and words that they blame you for this shortfall. And, no, it's not fair. Of course, if you've been paying attention, I never promised you 'fairness' on this journey.

I'm going to go so far as to say that this stakeholder's angry reaction is actually good. It means they understand you *now*, that they know you have a problem, and that they're paying attention to you in the moment. I hope you're prepared to take advantage of this moment, because it's a crucial one. This is where they will either come to see you as the kind of leader who is right for these efforts, or not.

How do you accomplish that? Well, a lot of this is going to sound the same as the section above. First of all, you're going to stay calm and not get angry or defensive. After all, you're disappointed that this issue/error/whatever has emerged, too – you're just experienced enough to know that these things happen. You're smart enough to explain what went wrong and what you're doing about it. You will be able to explain what different alternatives you explored and how you arrived at a decision. You'll be able to explain which teams/leaders are upset at the decision you had to make and what you're doing about it. And, you'll describe the processes you have in place to implement the change.

The culmination of all of these things is Confidence – you are exuding it, and they are learning that you have it. They may not reach the same level of confidence that you have, particularly in that moment … but they will observe it in you. And right now is the critical time where that needs to happen.

Sure, you told them there were risks involved in your project. You may even have been specific – and accurate – in what could go wrong. It doesn't matter – they will still react. It's what you do in that moment that defines you as a leader they will trust to keep moving things forward.

EXPOSING YOUR STARBOARD SIDE

It would not be profound for me to say "You've got to have some early wins in your project." I don't know what book first came up with that idea, but it was a popular one because even 22 year-olds who get assigned to projects will tell me "I need to get some early wins." So, that's good.

The problem I see is that this coffee-cup phrase and its repetition amongst leaders doesn't actually seem to translate into, you know, people getting 'early wins'. I have been part of projects that cost $80 million and projects that cost $80 thousand, and for some reason none of these projects are being built with a clear sense of what outcomes / capabilities / stories / returns were going to be delivered first, nor how fast. It's much worse when these projects involve IT[22]. (Note that this has gotten somewhat better with the recent advent of agile approaches to IT development, but even agile development gets compromised far too often. How many times have you heard people say "We're using a 'modified' Agile approach". Ugh.).

Let's take a step back for a second - *why* do you want early wins? What's the point? I think a third of people don't know at all. They just know that 'early wins' is what they were supposed to get, like a flu shot in November. Why did I print all these coffee cups emblazoned with 'Early Wins' on the side if that's not what we want, amiright? This glib approach makes it extremely easy to compromise on that ideal, which is exactly what Project Owners start doing when the going gets rough. Another third of people believe that early wins are a way of showing that the project is on-track and that they are doing a good job of managing. It's basically a mini-performance review, a way of either getting a pat on the back or getting your boss off of it.

Right or wrong, I tend to sit with the last third of leaders. This group understands a few things that resonate with me. First, especially for projects that involve IT, your executive leadership team has an inherent distrust that outcomes will be achieved. For example, if you go into your capital review committee meetings and tell your C-suite leaders that "I need $200,000 to upgrade our

---

[22] And I am in no way blaming IT for this. They often do their jobs well. I put this onus on the Project Owner.

payment processing engine on our e-commerce platform, which should take me 2 weeks", your leaders immediately assume at least 5 things:

1) This will take more than 2 weeks
2) This will take more than $200,000
3) At some point, something unexpected and bad will happen to our ability to accept credit cards from our customers and I will get *very* angry
4) Today, when you are here asking me for money to start this project, you are making this sound too easy, and if I knew the right questions to ask it would be obvious you're making a lot of assumptions. Later, when you come to ask me for more money, that's when I'll learn what I should have known to start with.
5) Even when this project is 'complete', we probably will not get everything you're telling me I'm going to get today.

Good project managers and innovators understand this paranoia. They also know that these leaders are correct – many, many projects have unclear outcomes. You will learn things along the way about your goals, your customers, your costs, your assumptions and your talent that will fundamentally change the project.

As I said above, the 'Agile' methodology is in part designed to help overcome this reality. I admire agile thinking and approaches. And, the one concept inside agile that should be adhered to rigidly is the idea of MVP – minimally viable product. Every sprint of the agile project should deliver a new MVP that enhances the last iteration in a delightful way and allows for rapid testing & feedback to inform the next sprint.

So, how does all of this affect *you*? Well, the point of all of this is that you, as an aspiring-effective leader of innovation must do two things. One is to avoid the 'long slog'. I name this after the concept of a treasure ship heading out to sea, its crew recruited with promises of career-building glory and its funding procured from angel investors given promises of large returns. But then comes the 'long slog' – that initial journey out across the open seas, which could take months (or years) just to get the ship into position for its first returns. Over that time the crew forgets the initial excitement from your opening pitch and just starts to wonder why the captain didn't pack enough rum. The investors, meanwhile, have too many chances to check their bank balances and be reminded that nothing has been deposited back to them in far too long. During that time – let's call it 6 months - both your crew and your investors get chances to hear about all kinds of other ideas, projects or concepts that will get them excited. Their desire to jump ship and follow something new and exciting returns over-and-over again.

You must not let this happen! Quick wins with product that can be released – even if minimally viable for the time being – should be seen as a set of increasing returns to all of your investors. It's more than just getting people off your back, it's a chance to show you can create *returns*.

EXCERPTS FROM AN INTERVIEW: "MARK", INNOVATION LEADER[vii]

Mark has worked in a variety of pyramids – HR, Finance, Markerting, Technology, e-Commerce and more – in his 15 years of corporate experience.

He currently works at a massive public CPG firm where, amongst his responsibilities, he is charged with leading and driving innovation.

Excerpts:

ME: What is your reputation at your company?

MARK: I'm probably viewed as an 'initiator'. I'm not somebody who spends his time reacting to problems around me – I try to be disciplined about spending 30% of my time initiating on opportunities that I think the organization should be capitalizing on.

ME: I'm surprised you can maintain the 30%.

MARK: Stephen Covey writes about the 7 Habits and being really thoughtful about what is urgent from what's just 'important'. [He talks about] Resisting the gratification of all the mundane problems you can spend 50 hours per week solving. I intentionally don't try to respond to every e-mail. I also try to spend no more than half my day in meetings. To do that, one of the things – just an example of how I clear space – if a meeting comes through and doesn't have a clear purpose or agenda, I decline it. They may come back and clarify the meeting's purpose, but often they realize there isn't enough content to justify having a meeting. Little things like that go a long way.

ME: That approach must earn you some reputational blow-back, though, right?

MARK: It could. My mindset when I'm starting fresh with new partners is that you solve some of their problems to establish credibility for yourself. You solve a lot of little problems. You hope that when it comes to making the big bets, the combination of what you've done buys you the ability to go for it. And then you hope that first big bet works out, which lets you dictate what you do and can't do going forward. If you're somebody who hasn't built that currency, it's much harder to do all that.

■■

ME: Tell me about people who might not have the clout you do in your organization. What's holding them back from being as innovative as you?

MARK: I think it comes down to trust at the end of the day. I was just talking to a colleague of mine this morning. We have a meeting with leaders where we're presenting a pretty significant innovation – basically, using all kinds of third-party data that will allow us to shift to more personalized marketing, rather than the broad marketing approaches CPG's have been using forever. For people who have done Marketing their entire careers, they are looking around the table at the people who are presenting and saying: "I don't know if I buy this idea. Do I believe in the people presenting? Do I feel like they're the right people to make this happen?" They are ultimately betting on you as an individual, not necessarily your idea. And people who come with those ideas, but without having established that confidence, see their odds of success fall.

■■

ME: What is the biggest risk you're taking personally?

MARK: Potentially alienating myself from some subset of the senior leadership team that has a lot of influence. If you end up on the wrong side of that track ... which can happen, by the way, even if you're having success. Even your success might be having a negative impact on one senior level person with a lot of influence, and it can send your whole project and career at that company into a spiral. That's the biggest risk. And it *will* happen at some point – you just have to be comfortable with it.

■■

ME: Let's say you got the green light on a project. What next? What do you immediately worry about surrounding yourself with?

MARK: Oh, shit! They said yes? [Laughs] From that point forward, I worry about making sure I've got the right people around me. It has to be a collective effort. You also need executive level sponsorship, because I think inevitably [without it] there will be hurdles that will prevent you from moving forward. You need access and sponsorship. And cover!

I also think, one of the things I try to do is be really clear about what success looks like at specific time intervals – short, medium and long-term. I want a toll-gate in 90 days where we can compare our progress against what we promised. If we said X, Y and Z would be done, are they? If not, what went wrong? Is this project not resourced? Is it just going to take longer? Do we change these success criteria or just kill the project? People need to see you are serious about stopping, if that's what's called for.

CHAPTER FIVE: A shiv and potable drinking water for two – *no, three*! - days

(Or, Tools you'll need)

If you're going to take this on, you can't do it alone. It's important you put every tool you can to work toward your goals.

Not every project is the same. But there are some basic assets that you'll want available every time you take on something new.

YOUR OWN ROUND TABLE

One of my best mentors taught me an important lesson. I'm going to share it with you here, and many of you will say "I already knew that". I bet you did. However, I'm assuming you'll continue to *not* actually apply this advice in your everyday work life, just like you have been (not) doing until now. Do you see how you are?

What I learned from this mentor is that all of us are imperfect and that we need to surround ourselves with talent. This is true not just on your team (although, that's a great place to start), but with peers from every part of the organization. Your round table must include voices from HR, Legal, IT, Operations, Finance and elsewhere.

Now, again, many of you will say "I already knew that". I get it, quit yelling at me! But what this mentor continued to teach me was that meetings don't start unless this *entire* group assembles.

What can we truly decide, he told us, if we don't have HR at the table to hear their perspectives? We all learned to be present at that round table meeting so real decisions could get made.

More: When we didn't act our part, he called us out on it. I remember a particular episode where I showed up to a meeting and a conversation began about delaying the rollout of our project by two months. Now, this project was near-and-dear to me and was going to save the company millions in expenses, so I was very interested in making sure it rolled out. As the conversation continued, it started to dawn to me that everybody in the room was talking to *me* rather than the leader of the project (and SVP of the organization who actually owned the business line). They were trying to convince *me* that the project's rollout should be delayed these two months. After I realized this, I listened for the better part of twenty minutes as they took turns making their cases. I thought their concerns were reasonable, so I said that as long as the project still rolled out, I was comfortable. That's when the leader stepped in. He said these exact words:

> *"Apparently, Brian's decided to be nice today. If the usual Brian had showed up, he would remind us that every month's delay costs the company $3 million. And then he would ask: Are your concerns worth $6 million, or can we find cheaper resolutions to those concerns?"*

Wow. In about fifteen seconds, he made multiple good points, but the one that stuck with me was this one: My *job* in that meeting was the represent the financial perspective of the decision and to give insight from that perspective. My job was *not* to make the decision, even if I thought other people were making good points. From then on, I reminded myself to Do My Job and provide that leader the valuable Finance insight he needed from me in that Finance chair. He, in turn, would listen to all of these points of view and make a hard decision if one needed to be made. That was *his* job.

To this day, when I assemble my own round table of leaders, I will pull them aside and remind them of what I need from them in each meeting. I want them to represent and advocate from their position and to make sure I have heard and understand their concerns. Only *after* we've all made a decision will we get in line and show unilateral support that decision, not before.

So, I ask you – are you truly assembling and using your own round table in this way? As a leader of innovation, the actions you are trying to take in the company are inherently risky both to your reputation and career. Are you utilizing the amazing insight of the people around you on a regular basis to understand your risks fully before decisions get made? Do *not* let them take away your decision-making power or even to talk you out of important decisions that need to get made, but *do* rely on them for your ability to understand the risks you're taking. This allows you not only to make the best decisions, but to take actions to mitigate risks.

THE RIGHT PARTNER

There is a tremendous book by Michael Eisner called '*Working Together*'[viii]. In it, he describes his relationship with Frank Wells, his long-time right-hand co-leader of Disney. Mr. Eisner also takes the time to review many other famous collaborations in business, sports and society. I strongly suggest this book for your reading list.

In (briefest) summary, Mr. Eisner suggests that strong leaders have strong partners, people they trust to turn to for guidance, counsel, venting … and even to be the people who will call them out on their own bullshit. He describes the difference in his own leadership style and effectiveness at the helm of Disney both with the presence of Mr. Wells and after his tragic demise. The frankness Mr. Eisner uses to describe not only his relationship with Frank Wells and the failings in his own personal leadership *without* Mr. Wells at his side are eye-opening, candid, vulnerable … and essential.

Read the book. Then, I ask – who is your right hand person? Who is the person who will:

1) … Help you avoid hiring mistakes, or call you out once you've made them (and, I'm sorry, we all will)?

2) … Be good at the things you're bad at? Maybe you're the strategist and they're the ones who communicate with the team. Maybe you're the disciplined project leader and they're the ones who pick up people's egos after you've abused them. Maybe you're the grand visionary and they're the ones who handle the fine details of negotiations.

3) … Be there for you when you're angry and let you get it all out in private? Great bosses understand that if they flip out, the teams feel that anger in a magnified way. If they're worried, the team freaks out even more. But, you're still human – you have emotions and you need to get them out. Do it in front of your partner – let them be your counselor, not the broader team.

4) … Privately tell you you're wrong, that you took the wrong stand on an idea or made the wrong bet with a resource. And, you'll believe them.

5) … Watch for your biases. Trust me, there are 'shiny things' out there that you can't say No to, and there are good ideas you'll never like. Their job is to remind you about it and to argue the opposite side.

There's more. But I'm here to tell you – people who have their collaborator well-defined are people who have (in my mind) a better chance at long-term success.

ABILITY TO CHECK YOUR EGO

If you start to be successful, there will come times in this project where people will start to give you credit. Resist accepting this, and instead make sure that credit lands with the people you will need throughout your career. That includes:

1) The leadership team that's most impacted – nobody is taking a greater risk in your project and innovative approaches than the leaders of the area you're disrupting. You are fulfilling your ambitions of being a disruptor. They actually need your project to *work*.

   But what's their reward for this risk? Obviously, you believe that the innovation you're leading is going to make their business run better, which more than likely leads to increased profits for their P&L. That's good! But there is a lot they are taking on in exchange for handing over the keys to your efforts.

   For one, they are *choosing* your project over others they might have otherwise selected. That business decision on their part is one of exclusion – certain things will *not* happen so your work *is* allowed to go forward. Granted, they are betting that your efforts will be lucrative, but it's still a position where they can be left wondering (at any point) if they chose wisely. Trust me, by selecting and championing your project they're doing you a greater favor than anything you're doing for them.

They are also dealing with blowback from the rest of their team. Trust me, somewhere in that pack is somebody who isn't a great big fan of your idea and reminds the leadership group frequently about it. More than likely they'll never say this directly to you, but if you ever see your leaders get frustrated during your project's 'down days', this is part of the reason why.

Speaking of down days, you're also making them deal with *that*. Every project will have rough stretches where things don't go well, additional funding is needed and timelines get stretched. During these times, you are (indirectly) asking those leaders to stand up for you in the meetings and conferences they have behind closed doors. When the CEO asks what that leadership group was *thinking* when your project got approved, it's not a pleasant conversation. They're defending *you* in those rooms. You owe them a lot for that.

I'll stop there, but that's not the limit of what they do to support you. When things start to go well, and when your product/project/approach starts to deliver … you had better be ready with how the story is going to show how these leaders are visionary and supportive. In fact, you had better be handing a version of that story directly to them so they are able to repeat it by heart!

To do this, think of 3 to 4 simple bullet points that summarize the risks taken, the vision desired and the outcomes achieved. Example: "[Leader X] saw that the industry was turning and that new competition was going to pressure margins. They invested in intense data-driven approaches to better understand their costs and how to control inventories. Therefore, they have managed to grow margins by a full percentage point in a market where our competition is seeing declines of 3-4 percent."

Something like that needs to be part of your project & communication plan. Arm your leaders with that story, tell it to your team, tell it to your stakeholders. Share it everywhere. Be brutal with the repetition of this story. It's important!

2) Your team – there is one critical word you need to remember about what you're doing for your team: Careers.

You are a career-builder. Yes, your team is working for you because they're excited in the project, excited for the company ... maybe even devoted to the company. That's great. But, ultimately, don't ever forget that they are not working for *your* glory. They come to work every day hoping to benefit themselves, their families and their career aspirations. They want more challenges and the chance to lead their own teams and projects. And, yes, *you* can make this happen for them.

To some extent (and depending upon your precise role in the company) you do control these outcomes. You have some ability to promote the talent on your team directly, adding to their title and their paychecks. That's the easy way.

I'm suggesting more. You also control the ability to turn the accomplishments of your team into *legend*. By sharing the roles each member of your team have taken and the outcomes they are achieving, you can begin to build up their importance to the company with people outside of your direct unit.

I'll share an example. I once took over a team that was considered very weak by the overall organization. The projects and outcomes they were delivering were considered to be low-average. It was not a team people wanted to work on. For those who worked on that team, they didn't understand how the work they did every day contributed to the company's mission. It was dreadful.

Skipping over the fine details, we began to turn this around. Part of how we accomplished this was by breaking down the drivers of our business and starting to understand how to get the organization to focus on improving those drivers. Influencing the drivers led to improved operating results. We were clearly on to something.

When it came time to talking about my team during annual performance reviews, I could have described the reporting they created, or the specific relationships they had developed. Instead, I talked about their strong conceptual understanding of how drivers contributed to the results of the company, and how they had shown innovation in finding new drivers within our business model and in how they went about presenting that information to leaders. I talked about how their presentations got leaders to *take action*, not just comprehend results (which is a *big* difference).

By moving the story away from the specific outcomes they delivered (reporting, meetings) I instead focused on the behaviors they were mastering. The thing about behaviors is they are desirable and transferable. My peers began to look at these employees as the kind of *leaders* who could bring these behaviors to their own teams. My team started to become *desired*, not just admired.

It all comes from blatantly giving away the credit for results to the direct team members who create them. Are *you* doing this?

3) Key owners of milestones – every project plan has critical milestones in it. It could the delivery of upstream components to a manufacturing plant, the completion of a module of your IT development, hiring goals, go-live dates or more. More than likely your project has milestones across multiple business pyramids, including Finance, HR, IT, Legal , etc.

In none of these areas – zero – will these milestones be easy to achieve. Problems will creep up. Work-arounds will have to be considered. Compromises will be made. You will depend on your leaders from each of these areas to get you to these milestones and beyond them.

Celebrate these wins. If you are on-time with a project milestone, make sure the owner of that effort knows that you understand this was a big win that she delivered. Make sure her boss hears about how appreciative you are. Describe her contributions and the challenges she faced so her boss knows that you know exactly how valuable she is and what it took to deliver results for you.

4) Finance – Obviously, I've spent a great deal of my career directly in the Finance function. I've sat alongside some great leaders and been part of projects and outcomes that made me really proud.

One day, one of these leaders sat me down and asked me a question. "Who is the most powerful pyramid in this company?". I answered two-fold: Merchandising and Operations, the two parts of the business that clearly had the most influence on the vision of the company. He shook his head. "Finance", was his firm answer. I was flustered by this – I did not *feel* powerful.

"Look," he continued. "Finance has the one thing we all need – money. Without funding in resources, project development and more, I couldn't do anything. Everything from buying the factory that will help us grow, to hiring the new talent that will run that new plant, to getting pencils for my team to use every day comes down to my budget and what I've been empowered to do. And that empowerment *always* comes back to money. Underneath every strategic conversation we have is money. And *you* provide it to us. And the reason I value your partnership as much as I do is that you have implicitly understood this during our time together. You've helped me connect with the right people to get my funding needs considered, you've advocated for that funding by sharing my vision and story, and you've help me understand how to control the various financial levers I have to manage every single day toward delivering outstanding results."

Later in my career, I had a chance to test this when I left Finance for the better part of a decade. I got the chance to have some Finance partners who were strong, and some that weren't. Some people became very invested in what I was trying to do as a business leader and advocated for what I was doing in rooms where I wasn't even present. Others just saw what they did as fulfilling basic Finance needs, like providing me with the specific reports I've ordered from them (and little else).

The bottom-line: You will never have a success in your career that doesn't in some way come back to effective Finance support and advocacy. Share the story that I shared with you above to let your partners know the importance with which you perceive them. Work hard to make that a productive relationship. And, when you deliver results, go back to them and help them tell the story of how their contributions led to real outcomes. It won't hurt.

THICK SKIN

You will be under attack. And, mostly, it will not be a direct attack. People will talk behind your back. They will tell stories about how stupid you are – most of them will sound a lot like "she doesn't understand [insert virtually anything here]".

Your approaches will not make sense to them. Let's face it – if everything you're going to do just made sense to everybody else, other people could and would have done it by now. No innovator would be necessary. The idea of building a great team, selling them on a powerful vision and then eliminating obstacles to that vision will sound too much like coffee cup logic to your peers. Of course, in their hands, it *would* be coffee cup logic! Regardless, they will criticize you for it.

So ... sorry, but welcome to leadership! Guess what, there's nowhere to hide in leadership no matter what you're doing. But, in particular, your innovative approaches will draw scrutiny.

Most of you do *not* have the stomach for this scrutiny. It will be personal and unfair and a distraction from what you should be doing. That's just how it is. Frankly, this same kind of ugliness is what separates people who can be CEO/CFO/CHRO/etc. from those who can't. It's the very reason why many, many people get closer to those corner offices and quickly realize they don't actually want those jobs. "I'm doing this in exchange for *money*?", you'll ask yourself at some point, and it won't feel like a fair trade-off. Only a small percentage of you will be able to crash through that feeling and keep going.

Most of you don't have it in you. You believe in things like 'fairness' and believe you should be judged on your merit only. Sorry, real-life doesn't work that way.

So, what do you do? First, understand that this is reality – there will be scrutiny. To counter-act it, you need to do some of the other things I've listed in this chapter, including managing the politics, have a 'safety cushion' financially in case you're actually fired[23], and have a great group of peers around you who can (and do) give you terrific advice.

---

[23] Yikes! Fired? Did we skip something? Don't worry – we'll get back to this in a few pages.

COVER FROM YOUR BOSS

Who is this person? I mean, really? Because to deal with the likes of you for the next 12-24 months while you try to pull this thing off that you're doing, it's not going to be easy.

Warning signs (for you) could include:

1) Are they the kind of person who reacts strongly to getting a difficult phone call?
2) Do they tend to follow all the rules?
3) Are they close to retirement and really don't need you rocking the boat?
4) Did they hire you with the intent of 'keeping the boat floating' rather than disrupting the operations?
5) Are they the micro-managing type?
6) Or, even if they don't come directly into your business on a daily basis, are they the type of boss who gives very specific directions on how things should get done?

Let's talk for a second about the business of 'you'. You, Inc. did not get in business to get your boss into trouble. You, Inc. did not get in business to get your boss fired. Of course not.

If anything, You, Inc. exists to get your boss *promoted*, or at least to increase the likelihood of that happening.

You may not explicitly start every day thinking about this, but it's indirectly true whether you like it or not. When your boss went through the interview process and made their selection for who would get your job, they were (in part) doing so based on what was best for themselves, as much as what was best for the company. Who would reduce their day-to-day risks by running a great team? Who would deliver results with the least amount of oversight required? Who could, some day, get them some praise for making such a great hiring decision? They came to the conclusion that this person was you. Don't screw it up.

So, what does 'cover from your boss' really mean? It means the most candid and personal relationship you have at work needs to be with your boss. That person needs to know the risks you're taking and needs to trust you. They need to know that *you* have their back and won't put them in an awkward spot where it doesn't look like they are steering the ship.

How do you do this? You make sure you're regularly covering the following items with them:

1) No surprises: If something is going wrong, you tell them about it. Immediately. No matter what it is, or how unimportant it may seem to you, you tell them. They may know about politics you're not aware of, and could help you (and them) mitigate risks.

2) Who's who of who's angry: Be specific. I don't care if it's the HR generalist who posts your jobs or the SVP of Finance, make sure your boss knows who may not be happy with you. At any time they may find themselves in a room with your partners, and they need to know ahead of time who may be hostile and why. It helps them stay calm in the moment and to think ahead.

3) Where you're weak and what you're doing about it: You suck, and they know it. Remind them of the areas of the project where you feel most vulnerable – perhaps it's your lack of experience managing large IT projects and your inability to tell if the testing being done on those modules is sufficient. Then tell them what you've done, via personnel or otherwise, to try to compensate for this. Your boss's

experience and network might come in handy in this situation.

4) What could go wrong: If there is a sizable legal risk, or union risk, or personnel risk, you had *better* be sure your boss is educated on it. Do not let the firefighting stage be the first chance for that person to find out what kinds of risks you were taking. No matter how remote those risks may be, be explicit and repeat them often. Just because it's risky doesn't mean you shouldn't do it ... but they need to be partners. Remember, you have much more information than they do, so while you may think a particular risk is well worth taking, don't assume they've thought it through as carefully as you.

AN ABILITY TO SELL YOUR STORY

If you're not talking about your project, somebody is. And you have no idea what they are saying – it could even be good! (HAHAHAHAHAHAHAHAHA! It's ... it's not good. It's not.)

A long time ago I had a boss who was frustrated about a project he was leading. I happened to be in his office and he looked at me and said, "These guys are angry at me because I'm making them stop their work to help me build a deck to communicate back to the Steering Committee. They complain because I keep asking them to contribute these stories – they think I'm *interrupting*! I feel differently – in fact, I don't even know why I have to *ask* them for this at all! They *should* have built Communication Events into their project plan in the first place. *Communicating is part of the project*!"

I believe he was on to something, and I've rigorously adhered to it ever since. An effective project must have routine points built into the timeline where you are out showing your MVP[24] to stakeholders across the organization. The value of this is simple but expansive:

1) It shows them progress is being made
2) It gives you a chance to remind them of the value of your project
3) It gives you a chance to re-pitch where you're going – "For now this app only allows for 4 key reports, but in Phase 3 we will expand to the full 10 reports"
4) It gives you a chance to remind those stakeholders that you're aligned to the BUSINESS NEED, not just running a project – "We would have loved to have had all 10 reports ready-to-go, but by releasing the app with these First 4 we will hit on our most urgent business needs, get a chance to get feedback during live production, and allow the team to better manage our inventories starting immediately"
5) This is a big one: It helps remind them of the power of the agile approach! Remember that most leaders are used to projects that, once the project has ended, they are left with tools that are flawed and (often) unfixable. It would take ANOTHER project to address the fixes, and they know the odds of that happening. You will have a chance to say: "By starting to get feedback on the First 4 reports, we can incorporate improvements to those reports into Sprint 4 of the project. If we'd waited until all 10 reports were ready, we would have had less time to make improvements."
6) It gives you a chance to tell stakeholders what problems & mistakes you've run into on the project. This gives you a chance to own & control the story of what's happening inside

---

[24] Minimally Viable Product, an 'agile' development term.

the bubble that is the project team, and prevents (or limits in effectiveness) any versions of those stories from being told improperly by others.

7) It gives you a chance to hear complaints from stakeholders face-to-face. Do not assume they will always take those chances in Steering Committees or other public settings. However, you *should* assume they'll take chances to gossip amongst each other if they're not happy with you.

The bottom-line here: If you are not 'filling the void' with your own story of your successes, challenges and failures, you should assume somebody else is. And, that it's probably not the story you would want told.

One other note: You should not always assume that even if you *do* tell your story that people will believe you or side with you. This is not about creating spin. What it is: A organized and coordinated chance for you to have at least put out your own version of what's happening, such that when leaders hear something contradictory they start by saying, "That's not what I heard."

THE RIGHT TEAM

Nobody is perfect, especially you. Keep that in mind as we go through these next sections.

Take a look at your C-suite. Let's be straight – these are some deeply flawed people. They have tempers. They do not seem to have a strong hold on the time-space continuum, or any other skills that would allow them to approximate how long something takes to get done. They're arrogant as hell (which, to be fair, is probably a crucial defense mechanism given how shitty their jobs are). So, they're not perfect either, which is actually GREAT NEWS! It means that you, too, could be C-suite material someday.

But, how and why? We've already established you're flawed, so how on Earth are you ever going to get these chances? For most of you (and I think I've been consistent on this) you're not. Give it up. But for a rare few of you, you just might! And that's because the things you're actually good at will make all the things you're terrible at tolerable.

Wait, what?

Yes, just like Uncle Ted at Thanksgiving ("He drinks a little more than he should, but he also serves at the local soup kitchen on holidays") your redeeming qualities may be sufficient to make up for the deep inadequacies you have. The balance between these things is key. We can tolerate Uncle Ted's 'foibles' because he is family and we see the good in him, too. However, if Uncle Ted upgrades to burglary, our tolerance wanes.

All of us have a litany of attributes that make up the entirety of us professionally. These are skills (Excel wizardry, an ability to drive a forklift, etc.), experiences (have closed the books at the end of the fiscal year, have gone through a merger, etc.), physical attributes (7 feet tall, ability to lift 200 pounds), knowledge (awareness of the tax code or laws governing unions) or competencies (great communicator, develops talent, manages projects efficiently, etc.).

So, this is a VERY large list of attributes. For some of these things, you will have no natural skill. For example, I cannot dunk a basketball or do heart surgery or assemble 1000-piece puzzles. I'm terrible in crisis situations – when something crashes or I see blood, I freeze for what feels like forever (ask my wife!) as my brain works through the situation. So, certain jobs are automatically ruled out for me. The good news is that most of these skills are not part of my day-to-day needs.

So, let's refine that list or attributes down to things that are relevant to my job, my company and my career. Within that, there are some real strengths that become obvious. I am excellent at recognizing trends. People tell me that I have strong communication skills, especially in situations where there is bad news to share. I am extremely focused and well organized. I have been known to recruit and develop great talent for the organizations in which I've worked.

There are attributes that stand out as weaknesses for me, too. I'm a little too quick to drop an f-bomb. I occasionally over-trust my team, such that situations can get farther out-of-hand than if I were monitoring more closely. I can underestimate how important some processes are to running the day-to-day operations of the organization. Even as a person whose career leaned toward Finance roles, I still have a loose understanding of SOX[25] and have never been asked to officially close the books at year-end (which can cause me to under-appreciate those roles). I'm sure there are more. The importance here is relative balance.

Let's try to visualize this. Looking at the chart below (Chart 5.1), assume the X-axis is lined with the extensive list of attributes (skills, experiences, physical attributes, knowledge and competencies) that could *possibly* be important in any one person's career. The Y-axis measures that person's relative skill along each of those competencies. Where the Y-axis crosses the X-axis will be what we'll call the 'expected' or 'desired' state of each attribute. For example, being able to construct a basic model

---

[25] Sarbanes Oxley Act, nicknamed SOX. It is not a reference to the article of clothing, with which I have actually become quite exceptional at wearing. All the hard work paid off.

in Excel would be expected of a Finance professional. The ability to manage massive data sets in Excel, or to write Visual Basic code for automating tasks, would normally be well above expectation and therefore rates higher on the Y-axis. The ability to build a Marketing program would not be expected of a Finance professional, so (and this is crucial) even if the Finance person were terrible at Marketing, he/she would still be effectively *at* expectations.

Let's do a made-up version of how an imaginary person's attributes chart might look. We'll call this person Jane:

CHART 5.1

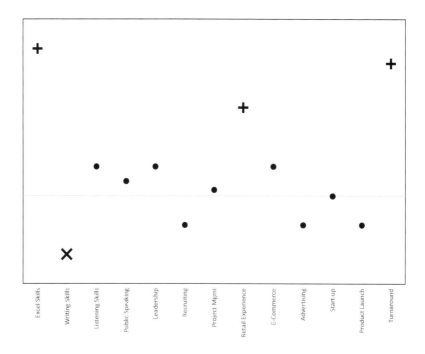

In Jane's chart above, all of the small dots represent skills & attributes for which Jane is so close to 'meeting expectations' that any differentiation, either positive or negative, are unimportant. For example, your assessment of her Leadership skills would say that Jane is pretty much on expectations for where she is at this point in her career. Maybe she's slightly ahead, but not so much that it stands out for her as a definable, differentiated skill.

Those items marked with a Plus (+) sign are skills & attributes for which Jane would be significantly above your expectations – in other words, in Chart 5.1 we're saying that Jane's Excel skills would be considered exceptional even when compared to her peers.

Those items marked with an 'X' are falling significantly short of expectations. Those items are also, by your assessment, important to the job. So, in the above, we're suggesting that Jane's written expression is important to her job and she is falling significantly short of what you need in the role.

Chart 5.1 shows that Jane, like most people, has a vast majority of attributes hovering toward the mean, or expected, state. What stands out for Jane are those 3-4 items items that are well off the expected state. These are those attributes that even the casual observer would look at and say, with even a small amount of time getting to know Jane, "This person is truly an outstanding example of that attribute." Or, for those items that fall well below the expected, or desired, state, you'd get the same feedback for Jane … just in the negative.

Why does this matter? Well, it matters exceptionally in how you construct your team, how you build complementary skills into your organization AND how you make the hardest decisions … who to fire. Without a framework, you can end up with middle-average players surrounding you and no ability to understand what actions to take. And those people *will* harm your ability for success in one way or another.

Let's shift to a new made-up person, Lana, and assume she is a sales person for a paper company. All else being equal, if Lana is out-selling the rest of her peers by a 10-to-1 ratio, she is an amazing sales person. Our theoretical paper company depends on sales to stay in business. I, the CEO of this paper company, enjoy both staying in business and getting a bonus. So I not only rate Lana very high on the attribute in her chart that is related to 'Ability to Sell', but I also *value* that skill much more than some others. For example, it may come to my attention that Lana is an absolute train wreck with Excel. Or, that Lana frequently submits the paperwork for her team's annual performance review late to HR each year. I will admit these attributes are useful, and that Lana's rating on these attributes is very low even in comparison to her peers … but I do not care as much.

Let's take a look at Lana's chart:

CHART 5.2

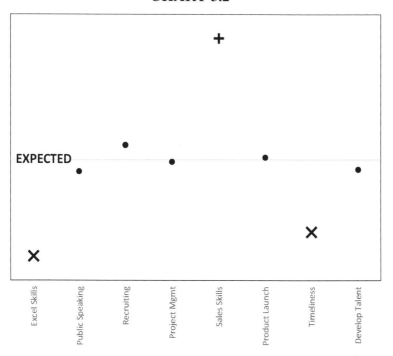

Here you can clearly see the trade-offs that are being made by Lana's boss. He is *accepting* that while Lana's skills with Excel and her Timeliness with paperwork are both *important* and not meeting expectations, her off-the-charts skill with Sales makes that up. Therefore, in his mind, Lana can remain an important person on his staff. Now, he may want to compensate for Lana's deficiencies by hiring a great Admin for her who can manage the paperwork, and/or send Lana to an Excel class. Regardless, by using a framework like the above, Lana's boss can at least understand the clear trade-offs he's making and *why* he's tolerating her obvious shortfalls.

Let's take this up a notch. Let's now assume Lana is bad at developing talent and I rate that skill for Lana as equally low on the Y-axis as I have rated her high for her sales skills.

Now, developing talent is important to me. The only thing better than having Lana on my team would be having 10 Lana's. I expect high level leaders to recruit and develop talent, and Lana is simply not doing that for me. We've had developmental conversations and I've challenged Lana to get better at this attribute, but she simply has not responded. It is not only a failure, but I'm very frustrated with Lana for this shortcoming. There's a lot that doesn't get done in her world because her team is simply not good enough and, equally important, not getting better.

Here's Lana's revised chart:

CHART 5.3

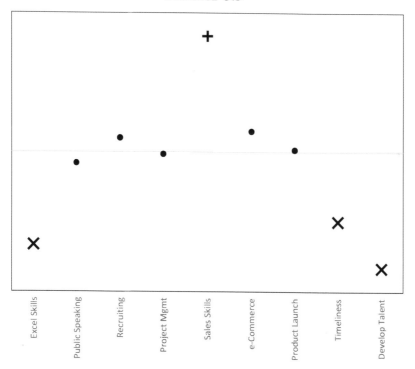

Do I fire Lana? I have to admit, it's getting less clear in this scenario. The 'reasons why I should keep Lana' remains obvious – because the value of what she *is* good at is so High and so important to me that I'm willing to forgive her shortcomings … to an extent. But the number and importance of the X's on this chart are starting to become conspicuous. Could this kind of chart ultimately impact Lana's ability to make the C-suite? I'm starting to think so! But, maybe not – remember, Lana is not just good at sales, she is *outstanding* at it. Maybe we can, at some point, compensate for all of this. But with the framework I'm using here, at least I am consciously understanding this trade-off and why I'm making it.

Let's make another adjustment to our chart. Now, let's say Lana's sales skills are only slightly better than her peers. She's good, but not outstanding. Everything else I described about Lana remains the same. Here is her new chart:

CHART 5.4

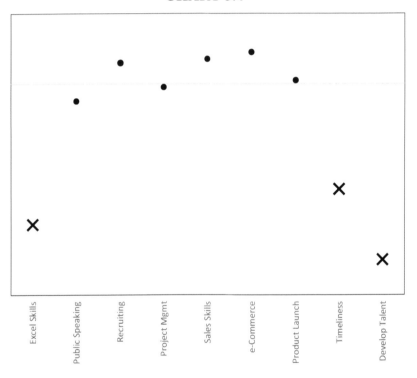

So, this changes things! Suddenly, Lana lacks that 'one big thing' [at least] that is differentiated and valuable to her boss. Suddenly, the significant deficiencies marked by X's on the chart stand out to me. As her boss, I may be less patient with her shortcomings and demand more. Note that she is not a *bad* sales-person in this scenario, just an average one. Importantly, she now lacks a killer app.

In this case, dismissing Lana needs to become part of my thought process because there is nothing to outweigh her severe (and important) negatives. I see many leaders tolerating significant negatives (the X's in Chart 5.4) while justifying that performance with examples from the 'small dots' on the chart. That's just painful to listen to. You're going to tolerate significant deficiencies because she is *average* at some of the things you want? When does that thinking end? You need to have an answer that question!

Let's do one more scenario with Lana. In this case, I'm going to cluster all of her attributes closer to the 'expected' line, with just as many above as below.

Here is that new chart:

CHART 5.5

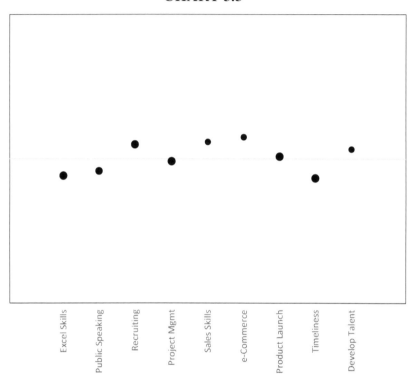

How many of you know somebody like this? They're good, but not great, at some things, but kind-of bad at other things. This would be somebody who, for example, has one of the better productivity scores on your team … but also might be more accident or error-prone than others. You appreciate that she gets more work done, but because she does you also find more errors than others make. None of these attributes is out-of-line an unacceptable … but nor are any of them exceptional.

These are the kind of people you wouldn't be crushed over if they quit … but you can't bring yourself to fire. They are "okay". There are 'C-Plus' players, and if you have enough of them they can just as easily bring down your team and your project as bad performers. As the Project Owner, you need to understand this … and understand it is *your* problem.

The bottom-line: The talent of your team is foremost. If you have not yet developed a method for assessing that talent, you are at a great disadvantage.

AN ABILITY TO SELL 'THEIR' WINS

It's not enough for you to be successful. In fact, it's not even close.

'Credit' is an interesting concept. To a person, you'll never meet a person who will admit to working toward a goal of 'taking credit'. In fact, I'd say 95% of people will even go so far as to remind you that they don't care about who gets credit. And, yet, and see if you can follow me here: human beings are tremendous liars whose (and this is well documented) pants are also on fire.

So, what I'm saying is, nobody wants to take credit, but to a person they want people to *give* them credit. Oh, they want it so bad!

This is much more than feeding fragile egos (though, that is important). For example – if you spend months reminding executives of why Jennifer Johnson is a superstar IT leader without whom the project would not be making the progress it is, at some point Jennifer's opinion on a key subject matter will have more power with those executives and will get an important decision made for you that otherwise might have gotten stuck in committee. You are *establishing* her power and ability to make those decisions, something that Jennifer may not have naturally had on her own.

Another thing – even if you do most of your boasting about your team and partners behind closed doors, don't believe that these conversations stay private. Word gets out. People know that you're supporting them, and they appreciate the extra effort. I cannot tell you the number of people I've sat in front of where I say something along the lines of "You are a really important person and I couldn't do this without you," and they stare at me like I might be trying to scam them. PEOPLE ARE NOT USED TO HAVING PEOPLE RECOGNIZE THEM AS TALENTED – they are not used to being asked for their opinions, they're not used to people telling them their performance is good (outside of review season) and they're not used to being flattered while at work. Initially they will distrust it, but eventually they will come to see you as somebody who genuinely cares about their output and will work to see them succeed in many ways. It's better if all of this is true because you're a good person and a good leader who naturally does all of this, but if not … fake it anyway!

So, your plan for this project had better include these steps:

1) <u>Establishing early with leaders who the key players on your team will be</u>: Okay, this is crucial for some surprising reasons. First of all, at this stage not all people involved with your project / initiative / distraction / event / disaster-to-be will think of what you've asked them to do in a positive manner. Like every person in every big organization, they have a day job and at least 2-3 'hobby projects' foisted upon them by their own leaders. In the beginning, they will not be able to differentiate your requests as being in any way special – you're just another jerk who's stealing their precious time. By setting the tone early on that you understand their role and importance, that

you understand the value they'll bring to the project and that you will talk about them openly as valuable, you give yourself a chance to set yourself apart. This, combined with later efforts documented below, is where you'll succeed in the long term. YOU ARE NOT THE SAME AS ALL THOSE OTHER PEOPLE – you're a better leader with a unique ability to drive success and make the people involved successful. Tone matters!

2) <u>Reminding people along the way who is being critical</u>: When your project first kicks off, build your communication and roadshow plan. Build an Excel sheet with all of your stakeholders listed in the rows going down the page, and all of the different tools you'll be using to communicate with stakeholders going in the columns across the top of the page. These communication tools can include things like e-mail newsletters, in-person status meetings with executives, surveys you would send out to check on people's impressions of your progress, steering meetings, lunches with key partners, etc. You would then go through this "matrix" and check off all the intersections – noting that certain stakeholders will get more than one communication tool. And, in these vehicles, always remember – RECOGNITION, RECOGNITION, RECOGNITION!!! It must be a priority for you that each of these tools *nail* this. Every communication should be a clear opportunity to define who you're recognizing and why they are standing out!

3) Reminding people as the project ends who was critical: As your initiative starts to take shape, there are two important steps. One is to Identify the Killer Apps of your project. What is it, specifically, that should be exciting leaders and

will ultimately drive the outsized results you've been promising? Is it the data engine? Is it the marketing pitch? Regardless, be clear what it is. The second important step is to start Identifying the Killer App directly with the Person Responsible. If that marketing plan is clever, start calling it Tonya Smith's Marketing Plan. If the user interface is going to revolutionize your industry, call it Mark Thompson's User Interface. Make sure Mark has a key role in showing it off. DO NOT LEAVE IT TO LEADERS TO MAKE THESE ASSOCIATIONS ON THEIR OWN – I know you might think some of these things are self-obvious, but like all human beings these people have a lot on their minds and they are not as good at connecting dots as you might think. Identify the Killer App, and literally name it after the Person Responsible.

4) Ensuring the organization recognizes those individuals after the project ends by forming the story of the project into *legend*.

Again, all of this effort needs to be part of your project plan, as essential to that plan as IT Testing, Change Management, budget and more. Build it straight into your timeline.

AN ABILITY TO BE FIRED

This is a sobering subject, so first let me say something to lighten the mood: Farts.

HAHAHAHA! Okay, now about the 'getting fired' thing – it's possible. Maybe likely. Especially if you're the kind of person who, as I strongly suggest *you* may be, should not be reading this book or trying any of these ideas.

The whole idea behind being an innovator is taking risks. Taking risks is risky (yeah, you paid for that thought – you're welcome!). As Scott Adams once said[ix]:

> *Risk takers often fail. So do idiots. From the outside, it's hard to tell the difference between the two.*

So, at some point, your boss may make the call that you belong in the latter group and should be purged.

It happens. Now, what about it? The point I would make is that, done well, there are outsized returns to being an innovator. You can command higher salaries for the work you do[26]. However, there are also outsize risks to having a gap in income. If you are consumed with the latter issue, you are going to naturally curb the former behavior. So, you should be the kind of person who:

1) Understands that risk taking and innovation are naturally risky, and that risky behavior should yield outsize returns, and has therefore asked for a higher-than-average salary as a return for taking those risks on behalf of your company. In other words, don't do this shit for free.

2) Has built up a war chest of savings. You want money sitting around in case you are (correctly?) called out for failure and let go.

Too real? Not the kind of 'fun fact' you were hoping to hear?

Ummmm … farts?

---

[26] See Chapter Eight for "Getting Paid What You're Worth"

EXCERPTS FROM AN INTERVIEW
"RICH" – IT EXECUTIVE[x]

Rich is a rising executive whose next role will likely be CIO level for his mid-size public manufacturing firm. He has worked for the company for 2 years.

He is struggling to move forward with new ideas, specifically machine learning capabilities that could drive new returns for his organization. In our interview, Rich describes a significant effort on his part to try to help others understand what will be required (funding, resources) to move the ideas forward.

Excerpts:

Me: You've described "them" as being too pragmatic and saying "That's not what *we* do". Why is that their perspective? Explain it from their side.

Rich: It helps to define the 'they'. I'm talking about the C-Suite. I think there's risk aversion. And I think the risk aversion is driven by … well, I think there is a short-term incentive on compensation that lends people, especially in public companies, to chase next quarter's results instead of results from 5 years from now. They say "Maybe that will help me in 5 years, but it's not going to help me next quarter, so I don't care so much".

Me: Are they right? Is [the potential financial return from your idea] 5 years out?

Rich: No, I don't think they are right, but how do you tell them it's 2-4?

Me: How *do* you tell them it's 2-4?

Rich: I don't know! [Laughs] Other than just telling them, "It's two to four, roll the dice!" [Laughs]

Me: It's not a very good executive pitch!

■■■

Me: On [your idea of machine learning capabilities], where are you going to be in a year?   What progress will you have made?

Rich: Today I have an idea.   Hopefully in a year … okay, it's not going to be one year.

Me: Where are you going to be in *one* year?   Where will you be at [with your project]?

Rich: One year?   We talked a little bit about the maturity process at the company I'm at today.   In one year, I hope to have a much cleaner data environment.   That's going to help us operationally. It's going to accelerate our ability to generate analytics.   It's going to allow us to push toward a dashboard environment we should have been at 10 years ago.   That's year one.

Me: Okay.   And then …?

Rich: Year two?   I want us to be looking at getting those dashboards out there.   Then, once I think we've done that and caught up – that's not where I'm aiming, but it's a step I think we'll need for credibility.   Then I want to see us get into that machine learning phase.   Boy … if we're not there in five years, we're dead.

Me: Let me change the question subtlety. I am the CEO of your company and I tell you "I love your vision, go. You have all the funding you need. Go." Where are you in *one* year?

Rich: In one year we have tools, data cleanup has happened and we're starting to dig into [the core project of machine learning]. I think we can get there in a year.

Me: So the "gap" to the value you believe is out there is in the neighborhood of 4 years, based on level of executive support you can achieve? That gap, that you're building into your timeline, is 4 years?

Rich: Yep. We'll be there in over 4 years, but could be there in 1 year if people were aligned.

■■

Me: What do you think it would take to change that variable [of time required to move your project faster]? What would be the event that would occur?

Rich: Some sort of shift, like the first iPhone was for mobile phones.

Me: Somebody *else* would have to do something? Some *other* company?

Rich: Somebody would have to come up with such a thunderbolt idea, a Moneyball idea. It's that, or a competitor eating our lunch.

CHAPTER SIX: Embracing your inner rampaging mother****er

(Or, how to get things done)

Okay, that title may be a wee bit over-stated. But you are going to face a lot of criticism. People will think you are stupid, incompetent, arrogant, reckless and worse. They may actually say that to your face.

Remember, it's not their fault. It's yours! Even if it's 'good for them' ... *you* did this, not them! You made it start, you said 'yes'.

So, before I dive into your behaviors and reactions, let's talk about *them* for a bit. They're pretty important here, and they're bound to have some outsized reactions to your efforts. I've made a pretty good career out of one simple saying: "Expect people to act like *people*, not like artificially enhanced change machines. Then plan for it." So that's what we're doing here.

THE PHASES OF CHANGE

You've got to have a way of organizing 'change' in your mind, some model you believe in. It needs to be concrete. It needs to be the foundation of your entire approach to handling people through the innovation you're driving.

I subscribe to the change philosophies outlined in a great book called '*The Change Cycle*' by Salerno & Brock[xi]. In it, they devise six phases that people have to go through in any organizational change effort. It's a brilliant book, and I strongly recommend it for all of you.

Rather than belligerently stealing from their materials, allow me to lift the concepts, convert them using my own experiences and approach, and (hopefully) land it in your conscience using a concrete example of those concepts.

I will use road construction as a proxy for whatever it is you're doing to your organization, because everybody hates road construction and, if you're the kind of person I think you might be, everybody probably hates your ideas just as much.

1. LOSS: This is the phase where you've been informed something is coming. "We are going to do road construction on Highway 100". It's not happening yet. You're not even sure what the extent of the construction is going to be, or how long it's going to take. But, you're now aware it's coming and you don't like it … but you don't *truly* have to deal with it yet. In this phase, communication is what's key. You'd rather not enter into Phase 2 without the vast majority of people being aware that change is coming.

2. FACTS/ANGER: This is a crucial phase – now your audience knows *exactly* what's coming. The construction on that highway is going to shut down the whole road and for more than a year. This will have dramatic impacts on your commute, and maybe even your ability to get home to pick up your kids at daycare dependably. You are *angry*. You know that there is a similar construction going on at the same time for another major North-South running road – have the city planners

gone completely crazy? There's only going to be one road left for everybody! This is a nightmare! In this phase, you want to let people vent. What I've always told my employees: If the phones are ringing with angry phone calls, it means people *understand*. That's good! The anger is not wonderful, obviously, but it means your message got through. It's only if the phones aren't ringing that I get worried – that means people didn't comprehend what I was saying. It means I'm delaying the anger.

Also, do NOT drop balloons and hand out t-shirts during Phase 2. Let people get their anger out. Don't keep reminding them that "things will be better eventually", or hit them with your slogans. The only thing you want to correct is if people are hearing myths or non-truths. If so, correct it. But don't sugar-coat the actual truth.

3. DISCOMFORT BECOMES PROGRESS: Like it or not, you're in the new world. Highway 100 is gone and you're making due. Don't get me wrong – it sucks. But people across the city have adjusted their schedules due to all the construction, and while traffic is *not* good … it's not as bad as your worst fears, either. You're not happy, but you're not as angry as you thought.

4. PERSPECTIVE FORMS: Okay, the new road is open. And … they fixed some things! They stretched out the on-ramps for a few critical roads, making it much easier (and faster) to get on this freeway. And, there used to be a bottleneck at one section of the freeway where the lanes collapsed from 3-to-2, and that's been completely fixed. That year of construction sucked, but the end-result does actually seem, dare I say … better?

5. BENEFITS: Okay, your commute has been cut from 45 minutes to 35 each way. It's way more dependable, and the more you use the road the more it becomes obvious that the new lanes are less susceptible to ice and flooding than they used to be, taking major variables out of the equation that used to be part of your life.

6. RESILIENCE: You made it! And, because you made it, you are now much more capable of dealing with future changes. Your trust levels are up, even when things don't get radically better.

I like the Change Cycle. Whatever change management process you favor, follow it. The point here is, you need to have one and it must be embedded (and scrutinized) as part of your Plan.

A PROCESS PEOPLE FOLLOW

I don't need much for this section, but it will be the hardest for you to implement. Here goes: When you ask somebody to do something, they need to do it for you. There. That's it.

If you're holding meetings on Monday afternoons at 2:00, people need to attend. If they can't – and this should be rare - they should write to you with their inputs ahead of the meeting and *not* just send a note saying they can't make it. Their contributions are expected and non-negotiable.

In order to hold those meetings on Monday, you need status sheets filed by Monday morning at 9:00 a.m. People should send these to you. If they don't, hunt them down. Make it awkward.

The point: I presume there is a lot riding on this project / initiative / idea that you're leading. People need to treat it, and you, that way. I know they have a lot going on, but this is one of those things. If you don't have control of the process, you will struggle. I know being the bad guy will make you uncomfortable, but get over it.

AN ABILITY TO MAKE DECISIONS

You can make decisions. Say it. You can *make* the decisions that need to be made.

As we have stressed (and will continue to do so), this should not be done in a vacuum and should not be done without asking for guidance and insight from people around you. But, at the end of the day, you may have to stand up and make the final decision. And, when that time comes, you will.

Here's what you will *not* do – ask permission to do this. Stick with me for a second – I know your every instinct is to probe and ask your leadership team about what decisions you can make, what decisions you can't make, etc. You want to know your own boundaries, particularly if you're new to all of this. Don't do it. Assume you can make *all* the decisions related to the project.

You are accountable, right? If something goes wrong, the buck stops here, correct? If so, then you can make the decisions that lead to those results. Don't sabotage yourself.

Okay, so we have a framework and elements that must be embedded in your Plan. It doesn't mean you're going to be popular, but it does mean you have a plan and you know what to expect. You're tenured. You're valuable. But you're not out of the weeds, and things-about-to-get-messy!

CHAPTER SEVEN: Black holes and other unpredictable problems

(Or, What can go wrong, and other things that *definitely* will)

Okay, so I think I've mentioned pretty regularly throughout this book that I have concerns with your idea to become an innovator. And, yet, here we are in Chapter Seven and you're still reading.

By the very nature of the work you're (seemingly, in spite of my advice) planning to do, things are going to go wrong. Now, early on in your career as an innovator, you won't have any experience with the calamities you will either directly cause or be adjacent to. You will not know what to do.

I once talked to a boss about this. I asked him, "Why isn't there any training for decision making? I mean, all of a sudden I'm running a team of 50 and a $100 million budget, and it's not like you built me up to this with smaller efforts along the way." He looked at me and smiled and said this:

> *"Brian, there's nothing you can do as a manager of a team of 5 that tells us if you can manage 20. And there's nothing you can do as a manager of a team of 20 that tells us if you can lead 50. And there's certainly nothing you'll do as a leader of 50 people that will tell us if you can handle 200, or 1,000 people. At some point, we just have to say to ourselves: You know, I think he can figure it out! Then we all take that risk together.*

*But don't worry– if it turns out we were wrong, we can
always just fire you later. "*

Hahahaha!   So encouraging.

Anyway, shit's going to go down.   You will have problems, and
they will not be simple.   What follows is advice on how to lead in
a space where things can and will go wrong, some of the attitudes
and approaches you need to adopt, and maybe some thoughts on
fall-out strategies.

YOU DON'T GO FAST ENOUGH

One thing to think about – many of the projects you will take on in
your career are vast.   They are deliberately set up to take years to
complete, and there's no practical alternative.   Let me just point
out how risky this is for you.

There is always excitement at the beginning of a project, and the
bigger the project is the more excitement there will be.   Even
projects designed to take *years* to complete will have this stage.
However, as numerous other books will point out to you, this
excitement will wane.   Eventually your project will *only* be a
drain on cash, attention and resources for the company.   You will
have had problems with budget issues, turnover of talent, and
constraints that weren't known (or understood) at the time you
embarked.   Those issues will be the most recent impressions of
your project in the minds of management.   And, every so often (at
least) somebody will bring up: Are we sure we should keep
pouring our precious energy into this project?

You should understand, these doubts that creep into senior
management's minds are very much as dangerous as a war ship's
cannons. They can sink you.

So, what do you do? First and foremost, no matter what your project is: You must have early wins. "But, Brian," you argue, despite the fact that we are not on a first name basis, "My cold fusion project won't even have the flux capacitors installed for 18 months. How on earth can we do anything before that?" Yeah, I don't fucking care. Get the flux capacitors installed faster. Get it done. You MUST deliver prototypes, or marketing materials, or customer analysis, or sales, or whatever in the first 6 months, period. Go back to the drawing board. Yell a little at the engineers that tell you 'can't'. Scream at the Finance people who argue about your budget. Again, I don't care. You must have consistent wins throughout this thing in order to attack the doubt that will set in from various points of your organization.

Or, don't. Run *that* version of the project. See what happens. I'll wait here, shaking my head.

YOU DON'T KNOW YOUR MVP

I've talked elsewhere in this book about the concept of MVP – minimally viable product (not my term, just using it for illustration). The concept is pretty clear, but let me expand on it with something people can relate to – the apps on your phone. Now, when the lay person starts thinking about building an app, they can't help themselves but think of all the things they want the app to do. If, for example, you have the idea for a new type of calculator, you also would like it to:

1) Be compatible with both Android and iOS
2) Be able to convert different currencies, and …
3) Connect on-line so it can keep track of currency fluctuations, which change daily

4) Sync with your calendar and e-mail
5) Be able to have different background colors or "skins" based on user personality
6) Be voice-compatible for people who need assistive technology
7) Work with the Apple Pencil and other input stylus options
8) And so on…

The thing about it is: Do people even *want* your calculator? I mean, if they reject the core functionality of this new device you're creating, aren't all of these other features meaningless?

But this idea of MVP goes beyond that concept. What I'm saying is: The act of trying to accomplish all your wish list items from above will add precious time to your development cycle, and that time is crucial for your credibility and the long-term funding of your project. Remember – you are not operating in a vacuum. You can lose funding or the company's interest in no time. I have seen many, many outstanding ideas that got stuck in development and never got published because the leaders got bored, or distracted, or just otherwise lost faith in your ability to ever publish. I've seen too many projects that pursued 10 'features' become unable to accomplish the 8th, which is what ultimately caused them to go over budget and way over timelines. And, suddenly – their funding is gone.

Your job #1 is to protect your funding. You worked so hard to get it in the first place – do NOT let it go. Throw yourself bodily over that stack of cash and do what it takes to keep it.

So – Publish! As the leader of the project, you must walk around screaming this word over-and-over again: "Publish!" Get something out the door and into the hands of the users or customers or whatever your audience is set up to be. Begin to build a base. Find out if your core product or idea is viable. Yes, some of your users are going to complain about the lack of assistive technology or personalization. If you get those complaints you're doing *well* - it means your users care about your product. Plan for fast follow-ups that can remove bugs and add a feature or two in each release. But don't let the fear of feedback or disappointment keep you from hitting the Publish button ASAP.

YOU DON'T PLAN FOR, OR DELIVER, 'FAST FOLLOWS'

'Fast Follows' in this case is when you plan for releases after your initial launch. In the case of reporting, it would be upgrades to that reporting that incorporate user feedback. In the case of IT projects, it would be literal iterative releases that fix bugs and add new functions. In the case of HR programs, it would be modifications to policy or process that incorporate feedback once you've seen how your organizations responds to the new directives. The concept works everywhere.

There is a hidden value to this approach. And that is this: How many companies have you worked for that *never* fixed their shit? 99% of their HR policies are the same as they were 5 years ago, even if most anybody could point out ways to improve. You're teaching all of your new team members the workarounds for the bugs in your software – you've even got little training guides with these cheats. But the bugs don't change. Things just don't get better, they don't get fixed.

What if your team suddenly started getting a reputation for the opposite? You build fast, you release often and things change & get better? It's typical in your daily life – think how often the apps on your phone get new releases! But at work, it's freaking mind-blowing if it happens! I *want* to be a mind-blower.

So, build your plan to Publish Fast and Fast Follow with iterative releases. And yes, that intentionally sounds like speak that works only in IT spaces, but trust me – it works in Finance, it works in HR, it works in Operations, and anywhere. It works.

YOU RUN OUT OF MONEY

I'm going to bring out my inner hypocrite here. This should be fun for both of us!

Out of the left side of my mouth I will say: You can't let this happen! You need to be in control of your budget and finances and see – well ahead of need – that you're going to have to go back to the Capital committee and ask for more funding. If you can't anticipate this, it means you're not in control of your project … and I can tell you from experience, that is *not* the leader I wanted to give *more* money to when I was running capital allocation processes.

Out of the right side of my mouth I will say: It's not so bad. Look, projects go over budget every day. It sucks. You get chewed out. I will quote the great Lt. Aldo Raine from the film *Inglourious Basterds*[xii]:

> *Col. Hans Landa: You'll be shot for this!*
>
> *Lt. Aldo Raine: Nah, I don't think so. More like chewed out. I've been chewed out before.*

Look, running projects comes with risk. Risk comes with getting in trouble and having to go and beg forgiveness. But you don't get shot.

Rather, I'm going to spin this around: What you *don't* want at any point is to *not deliver*. I would be much more worried about over-spending my budget if I didn't think my project was on track. But if I was over-spent and could proudly take my work-in-progress into the Board Room with me, then I'll take whatever budget over-runs come with it.

Far, far more often I see leaders adhere so closely to the budget that they kill their actual chances of success. Be successful first, and on-budget second!

YOU BECOME THE VICTIM OF SCOPE CREEP

Ah, my biggest nemesis: Scope Creep. Scope creep is, of course, the steady expansion of your project to solve new problems or challenges that you weren't aware of at the beginning of the project. For example, it could be simple: You were not aware when you took on the new ERP platform that you'd have to replace the servers in order to complete the installation. So, now, you have a rather complicated 'server replacement' project living within your ERP project. Scope creep!

Much more insidious is the 'want for more'. You start out by saying that you need a simple interface for end-users that asks them for 5 simple inputs and, based on that input, delivers them to certain reports. However, mid-way through your project, you start to see the value in adding 2 new questions to the mix. And, once you have all 7 inputs, you can actually do things with your software that you hadn't anticipated. Scope creep!

Another type of 'scope creep' is guilt-driven. You will have people who will come to you and tell you that your interface must be compatible with technology that allows access for the blind. Scope creep!

I'm not going to answer any of this for you. This is where you need your great 'round table' of advisors to step up for you and help you understand and interpret the challenges that are rising. Regardless, the more scope creep you can contain, the better off you are.

I *will* recommend this: Scope Creep should be put on its own template. You probably have a template you use for Project Management. You have a template for RAID. But Scope Creep should get its own list and be scrutinized by the Steering Committee during every meeting.

YOU DON'T PLAN EFFECTIVELY FOR CHANGE

Let me let you in on a little secret: You won't plan effectively for change. Nobody does. Ever.

You see, you can't possibly understand all of the ramifications of change. It just goes too deep. And, depending on the severity of the idea / initiative / project that you're driving, you can't possibly cover all of those variables. Even a great, great change approach will have gaps.

The first rule of effective change management should be this: 'Meet people where they're at'. It's a straight-forward phrase but it has a lot of utility.

First: you need to meet people where they're at mentally. If they are angry, your change approach had better address the anger. If they're excited but confused, you should address that. To know where people are at emotionally, you need to ask them – surveys and such.

Second: you need to meet people where they're at physically. If they are in the warehouses, I suggest you go there, too. If they are in separate HQ buildings, your approach needs to accommodate the different cultures of each building.

Third: you need to meet people where they're at procedurally. By this, I mean that some people want you to hand them an instruction manual and go away. Some people want a classroom setting where you instruct. Some need tangible training, where they are physically touching the new product. You cannot and should not force people across these borders – design training for all types.

Fourth: You need to meet people when they're ready for you. By this, I mean that sometimes the right time for you to do training isn't the right time for people to receive training. I was part of an M&A project once where we tried to teach all of our new employees how to use our Financial systems. Problem was, they were still working on the old systems trying to 'close out' their old company's books. We were so eager to seem helpful that we jumped to training too quickly. We had to come back once they were ready for us to teach them.

Finally: You need to design for adoption. If your goal is *mass* adoption, you had better have designed your idea / product / initiative / project for simplicity. If not, adoption rates will fall short of your goal.

If you are having problems with change, one of the things above is likely a culprit.

YOU LOSE SOMEBODY IMPORTANT

First of all – this is just the *worst*. I'm sorry.

You're going to feel a lot of pressure in this situation. If you don't, then it isn't somebody 'important' like I suggested above. Losing this person, whoever it is, is *going* to impact your timeline, budget and more. It's going to have an impact. All of these things will cause your inner monster to go into freak-out mode.

Here's what I can say: It's okay. Trust me, when you go to your Steering Committee, Capital Committee or otherwise to explain the delays and cost-overruns, everybody in that room will have heard it before. It's like being a new parent – everything you're going through seems new and scary to *you*, but to most of your friends and peers it's just another poopy diaper. They've heard the stories.

Don't hide from it, don't cover it up, and don't tell everybody it will be okay. Tell them the truth – this hurts. And, then, you tell them what you're going to do next. What is your plan? What do you need? That's what people want to hear from you.

NEW LEADERSHIP EMERGES

Okay – this is crisis mode. Take this very, very seriously. If either your champion or one of your key stakeholders at the leadership level turns over, your project is at risk. They will never say it, but *of course* it is. You need to get on this person's schedule and get them educated ASAP.

What do they want to hear? Of course they'll want some background on the project, its inception, its timeline, its outcome and more. But here are things they are really going to want to know:

1) How long will this take? Even if they ultimately support your project to continue, they will want it done so they can get their own initiatives up-and-running. They did not come into this job with the passion to close out their predecessor's initiatives.

2) How many of my resources is it consuming? How much of their team's time is going into supporting *your* work and *your* project? They have ideas they'd like to get stirred up, and again – even if they support your work – they would like to get their own projects started.

3) How much is the 'problem' that started this project aligned with my top issues? Is the initial issue that started up your project still an issue to them? Take the case where the previous boss simply would *not* listen to the CEO's concerns, which got him fired. The new guy will, of course, have heard this message coming into the job. If your project doesn't sound like it solves *that* problem, don't expect much support from the new guy. The last thing he wants to do is appear 'tone deaf' to his new boss.

In this case, don't worry about your budgets, your timelines or anything. Your entire focus should be on re-setting with this new executive.

SECTION THREE: IS IT WORTH IT, AND CAN WE MAKE IT BETTER?

In this last section of the book, we're going to try to look at the challenge of being an innovator inside large companies from two different angles. First, we're going to look at it from your point of view: Beyond the scope of any one project or initiative, how do *you* turn this innovative approach into an exciting career path? It isn't easy. Second, what could companies do (but won't) to make all of the innovation they purport to want happen much easier?

So, I'm going to talk about:

1) What a career looks like for somebody like you
2) Half-baked ideas that your company could use to improve the pace and effectiveness of innovation inside its 4 walls

EXCERPTS FROM AN INTERVIEW
"MARTA" – LEADER OF INNOVATION[xiii]

Marta is a mid-level executive at a $20 billion public company. Her career has grown rapidly in the last 5 years because of her ability to push through very large, complex projects and to build the type of teams that allow her to achieve those results. Her ability to understand the value and goals of projects at a very strategic level, and yet to understand the details of what it takes to make things actually work, set her apart from her peers.

Her largest frustration is always with pace, and the work it takes to actually get projects moving and to keep them moving in the face of bureaucracies that companies put in her way.

Excerpts:

ME: Why won't you achieve your goals in the next year?

MARTA: Distractions from projects. If my team gets sucked into the 'new problem of the day' – "Oh, this is our new corporate initiative", and we won't be able to focus to learn how the business processes relate to our work. It takes time, and they don't seem to be interested in how much time it takes to really understand the problems in order to be effective. In the word that we do, it's important to understand the foundations of how things work and to fix those foundations.

ME: Right.

MARTA: I think another piece could be team members leaving. That could lead to people leaving, key people [whose loss] would slow us down.

■■■

MARTA: The priorities we put in place when deploying are accuracy, performance and timeline. We will always cut scope in order to get something out quicker.

ME: What's an example?

MARTA: Last year we deployed some tools that were missing key elements that were obviously going to be needed by our end users. Of course, during the pilot we heard about those things. We knew people wanted those things. But, we didn't stop the launch because we felt what we had was good information and it was important to get the tool out there and to get people using it. And we just told them: "Here are the things we heard [about what you would ultimately want in the tool]" so they knew we were listening. But that fit into our other message at rollout, which was that this was Version 1. We're going to continue to listen to you and get your feedback and prioritize what you want. And those changes helped us build credibility.

ME: Did they believe you?

MARTA: I don't think they did, at first.

ME: Right, about whether you were actually coming back?

MARTA: They were used to new tools being deployed, and then everybody disappears. Anything wrong with those tools, they just had to live with them. And, so, we held training sessions, we had feedback sessions, we had change advisors and super-users that we kept getting feedback from. And, then we released [another Version]. And we continued to have a process of releasing enhancements and asking questions, and then leveraging that feedback to enhance reports and create additional reports.

ME: And, so when you went back in those first couple waves of improvements, that people were surprised that "She came back!"

MARTA: It was only 2 months later that we came back and added new data. [For things we couldn't do] we made sure to tell them that "We heard you", and we shared with them a roadmap of how we might go after those in the future. I don't think they expected that. We got notes saying thank you …

ME: Oh!

MARTA: … And it's not the culture that does that sort of thing!

■■

ME: As you build your career, what concerns you?

MARTA: I need to find something that aligns with what I'm good at.

ME: But how do you find that out?

MARTA: I'm looking for a place where I'm adding value to the company and growing as an individual.

ME: But how do you find that out?

MARTA: I guess you have to do it … I don't know that you ever know before you … it's a feeling. You have to take the leap and give it a try. It's be nice to know going in that you're going to be successful at it.

ME: That's not what I'm asking. I'm asking how you get your 'feel'. How do you *test* if the company is right?

MARTA: Asking good questions, I guess. [Clears throat] Trusting your gut.

ME: How nervous am I making you with these questions about growing your career?

MARTA: Very nervous! [Laughs]

ME: Well, let me ask you this: What kind of a conversation [would a prospective company need to have with you] that would make you say "Oh, they get it, and they are looking for *me*!"

MARTA: It's the "We got a problem. We have this thing that we're trying to solve. It's big, it's meaty, it's impactful, and we just don't know what we're going to do with it. If you want to make a meaningful difference to this company, we're going to need somebody who can build a team, focus on culture, driving real change at this organization …" I think them identifying the problem tells me they *get* it and they see the problem.

CHAPTER EIGHT: It could, *maybe*, be worth it, but probably not, but maybe!

(Or, Career opportunities and risks of being this 'maverick' you want to be so badly)

I feel like I've gone out of my way to emphasize that this is a non-traditional career. It's attractive because the thought of it can be very sexy – 'blazing your own trail' – but the thing you have to understand is that there's a reason some things are labeled 'non-traditional'.[27]

So what's the upside? Strangely, it's the same (but different[28]) as any other career path. You are building experience in a niche capability that can be extremely valuable to the right people. Same as building your resume on tax expertise, or search engine optimization, or in M&A work … being an experienced innovator in a large organization is extremely hard to find when you need it and SO valuable to the right person. Done correctly, you will have a career filled with an ability to demand premium salaries for employers to get access to your expertise, not dissimilar to consultants.

But, before I go much further, let me paint some foundations that will help with my later argument.

---

[27] Example: "That was sure a non-traditional way to get down the stairs. Now, somebody call him an ambulance."
[28] As always, you're welcome for this blast of clearly articulated insight.

PERFORM VS. PROFIT VS. TALENT

Let's start by making a broad assumption here – you are not the type of employee who is underperforming, or otherwise might fall into the 'Bottom 10%' in your organization. If you are, trust me – the world of Innovation and risk-taking is truly not for you. (I can't believe it took me until Chapter 8 to bring this up! This was a lot of unnecessary reading for you. My bad.)

It's also important that you are *not* the type of employee whose performance would be deemed 'acceptable' by leaders, but not crucial or exceptional. I get it – you get a task and you get it done. Also, you have ideas! About how things should be! If somebody would only give you a chance! (See later in this chapter – "What's in it for them?")

In any case, I'm moving along to the classes of employees that I would bucket into three categories: people who 'Perform', people who bring 'Profit' and those who drive 'Talent'. More on each in a minute …

… But first this fancy graph I made!

CHART 8.1

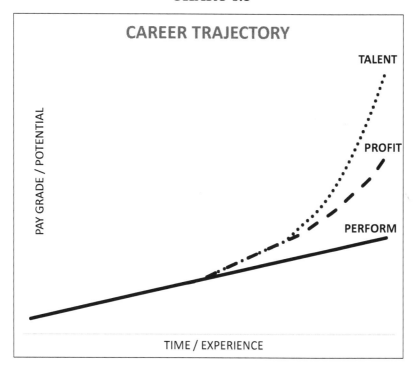

Let's start with the bottom line: **Perform**. People on this career path are those who, even for a very large company, you absolutely *can't imagine* living without. They not only get things done, they have a passion for the business, they continuously improve their skills, they move your business forward, they know your product inside-and-out, they know how to navigate your company to get things done, and so much more. They may, however, fail to be charismatic, or they may not enjoy the requirements of hiring-and-firing people, or they simply may not be strategic. But your core profitability depends on these Perform-ers.

People who Perform do have a trajectory in their career that allows for continuous growth and promotion. You can and will find

Perform-ers who are VP's. It's just that their trajectory seems to take longer than others, with more rotations, roles and time between promotions. When they do get promoted, it tends to be situational – they are absolutely the right person for a specific issue, they have unique qualifications or they are selected by a former boss who has experience with their performance and trusts them specifically and implicitly. The important fact here: people who Perform *do* get promoted!

In my experience, very large firms have a very hard time separating employees along this Perform continuum from the many, *many* 'just acceptable' employees (or, even, 'underperformers') that do their jobs but provide far less value. This comes from fear – many managers are afraid of the conversations they'd have to begin with their employees if they did attempt clear separation.

But I'm not talking about a firm's assessment practices here – I'm talking about *you*. We need you to have a hard internal conversation to identify where along these three continuums you fall. So, let's continue!

People who fall along the middle line, or **Profit,** on Chart 8.1 are those who, at a certain point in their career, start to get noticed as being capable of driving exceptional results for the organization … with the crucial qualifier that these results are deemed of *crucial importance to the executive team*. They create new businesses and new product lines. They turn around declining branches of the organization. They grow profit margins, develop interesting ad campaigns, design programs to optimize the company's tax liabilities, or more. And it doesn't always have to be straight-to-the-bottom-line value that gets lumped into this Profit category – employees who are exceptional at recruiting the best talent, or raise the company's standing in the community, sooth the egos of the delicate investment/analyst community or provide access to important government sources can also be categorized as our 'Profit-eers'.

Things that do not fall into this bucket (and here I'm going to be brutally honest, and I'm very sorry, some of you are my good friends):

- The best accountant
- Internal communications
- Trainers
- Payroll
- HR Generalists
- Programmers
- Project Managers
- Customer service or call centers
- Procurement
- Construction & architects
- Financial analysts
- Process experts

Yikes! I look forward to the rotten tomatoes that are assuredly en-route via express mail, what with so many of you being exceptional Type-A task managers in the categories above. Allow me to try to be clear, then: this does not mean these roles are not important, nor that they cannot pay a fantastic market value! In a large company, the best accountant (who I hope is your Controller) could pull down $300k per year or more. Kudos! And, for these people, I certainly don't want you to feel my hands on your back pushing you away from your company – you play an important role, and your work is valued. It's just that this work is not likely to have elevated beyond that 'Perform' line and reached the faster track that is 'Profit', where the slope of your career will be steeper with less time between promotions and significantly shorter, purposed roles designed to help give you experiences that allow the company to benefit from your leadership.

One of the most frequent things I hear from people who consult with me on their career is that "We should be judged by our performance, by what we've accomplished". These people look around and see others moving faster and getting opportunities to which they simply are not being afforded. My answer to this plea for a meritocracy is always: Are you nuts? You *are* being evaluated fairly! Your annual review and raise is based on your performance in your role. Most large companies even have a process by which they review people like you to ensure the market price for your talent hasn't changed (in which case they need to make a salary adjustment). Or, simply to be sure they don't lose you, they might move you more quickly to the top end of your salary range.

But you are too closely associating your *performance* with your *potential*. These are separate things! And the people getting other/faster opportunities than you are being selected for *that* aspect of their skills and performance, not their day-to-day deliverables.

I would assume that not a lot of people truly make it to the 'Profit' line in their careers, even though many companies are tremendously top-heavy on their assessments of who truly is. Maybe 10% of the people around you should be identified in this way. Probably 50% have been told they are.

Finally, let's talk about the top line in Chart 8.1, or the **Talent** line. To get here is very simple, but rare: You are not only the type of person who can deliver Profit to the organization, but you are the kind who can identify, develop & nurture others who make it to that same Profit assessment, such that the company's performance grows because it has many more Profit-eers than just yourself.

For example, you have consistently shown an ability to deliver above-average profit margins for the product line your company manufactures. As you do, you have hired and developed four other leaders who've gone off to other product lines and they, too, are delivering exceptional profit margin performance. Your ability to multiply your own effect not only singles you out differently from the very talented people on the Profit line, but it sharply increases your trajectory. People like this are often on the CEO track.

So ... where are you? The answer to that question will ultimately influence the promotions you receive and the pace at which they arrive. You need to understand this, and you need to test it with peers and leaders by asking hard questions. The next section of this Chapter covers exactly that.

ASSESSING *YOU* ... AND WHY YOU'RE PROBABLY FOOLING YOURSELF

Imagine standing in front of a group of 100 employees, all of whom have been pre-screened to be your best talent. Of this group, we should expect about 90 to actually be on the Perform path (remembering that this does not mean they won't get promoted, just that their path will be longer between promotions). Another 8 or so would likely be Profit, with 1 or 2 actually making it to the Talent line. Remember, these are 100 of your very best people, but natural selection at these levels can get pretty intense!

Now, let's ask the crowd! What we find is that in this example, more than two-thirds place themselves on something other than the Perform line. Not many are inclined to go all the way to nominating themselves as being on the Talent path, but it's still way more than will actually ever play out that way.

Wow! What a disconnect! Granted, this type of result would play itself out anywhere – a group of basketball players, a group of teachers, a group of electricians, etc.. People by their nature tend to over-estimate their abilities in relation to others. But, that's the point – self-assessment is not natural, so let's dig into this together … it might get a little bumpy.

FINDING YOUR PROFIT STORY

Building a career in the traditional manner is not easy, but does come with some straight-forward elements. If I would like to be the Controller of this large organization, it certainly helps to have a resume that starts with something like Junior Accountant and shows a progression of roles & responsibilities up the chain: Senior Accountant, Accounting Manager, Director of Accounting, etc. You probably need some cross-team rotations to help fill out your experience – Fixed Assets management, perhaps Inventory Accounting, maybe some time in Treasury or a rotation in Planning & Analysis to round out your skills. The point being, well-roundedness in this situation is a series of experiences steadily preparing you for higher-and-higher roles of the same variety – Finance and Accounting. It's a career path that to leaders of that organization will seem familiar and understandable – they can predict (and plan for) career moves that you'll want and need. Based on their own experiences they can assess your readiness and potential for leadership.

Alas, this will *not* be the case for you, my fellow intrepid non-traditional innovator! You know that you want your career to grow, but probably cannot specifically point even to the pyramid you ultimately want to end up in, much less a specific job title. Think of it this way: If you are a fantastic Knight of the Round Table, your next job opportunity isn't going to be found by looking around for a Senior Knight position … it's going to be found by somebody pointing you toward the next battlefield.

So, what do you do? As I see it, we need to flip the script. In the metaphor above, you need stop describing yourself as: "I work as a Knight in Camelot, one of 12 of the Round Table, 20 years of service to my kingdom and 12 years of knighthood." Instead, I think the words you want to use in building your brand are: "I fight, and I do it well. But fights are won and lost by teams of people, not individual Knights … no matter who they are. Over the years I've learned how to assemble those teams and be part of those teams. I've learned how to share wisdom and motivate people. The people I train go on to assemble their own armies. That's why you want me involved in *your* battles."

Perhaps it isn't obvious at first, but there's an important distinction between these two scenarios. In the first, the role itself is qualifying you for consideration for the job at-hand. You want to be head of Merchandising? What Merchant roles have you had that would confirm you can lead, develop, strategize, hire, fire and generally succeed in this role? If you have been growing your career in Human Resources and have been praised continuously for your versatility & intelligence, that still doesn't qualify you to be head Merchant.

However … let's say Merchandising is an absolute mess of an organization. The most recent SVP was fired for incompetence. Morale is at an all-time low and your most talented team members are exiting the organization. Nobody understands what success looks like. Politics are running rampant because, in the old regime, this was rewarded behavior. Now, let's say that you just dealt with that precise situation in your time in HR, and before that you faced the same thing in the Operations team. In every case, you were incredibly successful in spite of your lack of 'expertise' or depth-in-field. Rather, you have an eye for talent and a voice that gets people energized and aligned. In that case, you may very well be tapped for the Merchant role! In fact, they may not have anybody else for the job, because the next most qualified candidates at hand were products of the old, despised regime. *Not* having Merchant experience may, in fact, be an asset for you!

In this case, the interview will sound very different. You need to walk in with your resume, hand it over and say: "You're not going to find Merchant experience here. You don't need a great Merchant right now. You probably have the talent you need within your organization, but you're not achieving your desired results because what you're most missing is alignment. I've heard your story before, and I've tackled those challenges many time. I've done exactly this work in my last four jobs, several of which happened in different pyramids than HR. I'm a turnaround expert, and for the next 3 years I think that's what you're going to need. At some point we'll turn the role back over to a Merchant expert, and finding that right person is a big part of my job for the next few years. But for now, the skills you need have little to do with Merchandising."

With that story, I bet you get considered for that job.

DIFFERENTIATED – VALUABLE – TRUE

The reality is that most of us do not end up getting to realize our potential. Sorry! The vast, vast majority just simply pull up short, often well short, of what they actually could be capable of delivering. They just never get the chance to even fail, much less succeed. Why is this? Simple: Because nobody wants to give them that chance.

Read that again for a second. People naturally believe that to become CEO of a business, you need to do all the little things along the way. Mail room, junior analyst, junior executive, senior executive, maybe COO or CFO for a while. Right? Oh, sure, there are exceptions, like the boss's kid, who skip ahead. But the real track is the long play, right? Earn your stripes!

NO! Look to the boss's kid for advice here. Why did the boss's kid get to skip all those steps and start getting groomed right away? Because: somebody (ie, his dad) wanted to do that for him. Right?

And therein lies the big secret. The key to getting a job – ANY job – is for someone to *want* to give that job to you. If you're not doing the things that would make someone want to give you that job offer, then you're not doing the *right* things, you're just doing things. And, like most people, you're probably going to pull up short and miss your potential.

When I see somebody who is struggling because they're forgetting these simple facts, I always try to pull them back to it. What would it take to make that person *want* to give you that opportunity? Do you know? Have you asked? Are you focused on that? Are you *obsessed* with it?

Don't forget promotions! Oh, the number of people I've run into who believe they are entitled/due/ready for a promo, that they've delivered something great and it's the company's turn to do something for them. HAHAHAHAHAHAHAHAHAHAHAHA!, I say.

So, again – what's the difference? What gets people to want to do that for you? One thing, of course, is urgency. If there is a sense that you are marketable, networked, valuable and available, there is always more urgency in making sure you get yours. That, of course, requires a lot of work from you. I mean, you *technically* have to be actually marketable, networked, valuable and available to pull that off. That means you have to put time and energy into that. And the vast majority of you – 99% - do not. That makes you suckers for the company, and they love that. Good for them, bad for you. I don't care if you just pulled off a $1B win, don't expect more than a Meeting Expectations on your next review unless there's at least a chance you might run off and do it somewhere else. Your lack of effort on that front has made it obvious to them they can reward you at their own pace.

So, let's assume you are working the network to ensure you retain an element of urgency and you have a sense of your true market value. How is you most likely to be successful in doing this? Simple: Your personal story would have to be one that resonates on three elements – it's differentiated, it's valuable and it's true.

Let's explore!

DIFFERENTIATED: Whatever it is you do, that really defines you, must be unique. Are you great at Excel? Too bad – that's a dime-a-dozen skill. Interns have it. Are you experienced in international sales? Do you understand M&A tax implications? *Now* you're on the right track – it's hard to find those people.

VALUABLE: Whatever your answer is to DIFFERENTIATED above, it better be valuable. And, it better be valuable in the eyes of the person doing the hiring. For example: "I turn around divisions. My last six jobs were about being placed into roles where the shit had hit the fan, and my needing to work that team/division/company out of that situation." Whoa – that's something people will pay for!

TRUE: Whatever you said for DIFFERENTIATED and VALUABLE above, it better ring true and be exciting. This is why we have resume's and when you should bring that resume into the conversation. So many people lead with their experiences and expect the reader to make all the connections. "Whoa!" They expect the recruiter to say when reading their CV. "This person's run of experiences would be the perfect fit for that role we have in Marketing, even though his experience is actually in HR and Finance. It's the same kind of problem! We should get him in immediately and offer him all the money to get him to say Yes." This never happens. YOU have to make that connection for them, and then use your resume to back it up.

THINGS YOU'D BETTER BE DOING

So ... we've established that your career will not follow traditional paths. You may find yourself switching functions, and maybe even pyramids, on a regular basis. You'll often find yourself in situations where you are plainly not the SME (Subject Matter Expert). But that's okay, because for the things that *you* do there is nobody better.

Except, of course, for the fact that nobody will really know this about you. And, therefore, they are very unlikely to actually give you these opportunities, even if they should.

So ... thanks for reading! Have a great weekend.

...

...

Still here? That's weird, that's usually where I lose people. Huh. I guess I'll go on.

The problem is that people, especially leaders, are not in your head as much you'd like to think. They have a hard time remembering your kids' names, they've long-since forgotten that great outcome you delivered back in the Spring and they spend very little time wondering what you're thinking.

They don't even remember the bad things! For example, you may believe that your boss will *never* forget that embarrassing time you were up on stage giving that presentation to the entire Marketing team and had to pause for what felt like *forever* because you forgot where you were. Guess what, they don't remember that. They barely noticed it in the first place.

In this similar vein of barely paying attention to you, they also haven't spent much time dissecting your performance to pull out your core strengths and talents. Sure, if somebody came along and said: "You know who's really great at energizing the team? Jane!", they might just pause and agree with that, especially if your name does happen to be Jane (if this is a conversation between your highest-level leaders, then I'm not making any promises).

My point is: they are not experts of *you*, never will be, and truly spend an extraordinarily small amount of time actually thinking about you at all. There is only one person who is *potentially* an expert on you, and it is: You. And my experience tells me that the vast majority of you actually suck at this and don't really know yourselves well enough. But it is something you can get better at, and I'm here to tell you that this is really, really important if you're going to get the kind of opportunities you'd like through your career. And the reason it's important is that you MUST make yourself easier to remember, and in particular you need to make that thing you do best *extremely* easy to remember. In short, this is about your personal brand, and you need one.

Like I said, most people will fail to truly do this. How should you go about it? Well, start this way: Go to 10 people you know around the organization and ask them to give you three words that best describe you as a leader. There are really three ways this exercise can turn out:

1. Everybody pretty much agrees on one-or-two words that describe your strengths as a leader, and this agreement is something positive, unique and valuable to the organization. This is ideal. You will probably not land here, but it's where we aspire to get to.

2. Everybody pretty much agrees on one-or-two words that describe you, but those words are useless to you. For example: "tall". Or, "fair". Or (unfortunately) "smart", "punctual", "determined", or "hard-working". None of these words is sufficient to differentiate you or isolate those opportunities in the organization where you (and, ideally, ONLY you) are the best candidate to solve that problem.

3. There is no pattern in people's responses. You are getting some to say "change leader" but others to say "friendly" or "experienced". This is least ideal for you, but almost definitely what you will learn.

As I've already alluded, number one above is the ideal landing point. It is your clear brand to the organization, it is what people think about when they think of you … and, alternately, it is the set of problems where they'll think of you first when deciding who to pursue & promote for big opportunities. Again, in an ideal situation when a CEO is sitting around saying "Who do I know that can get this new product through start-up?", your name will be one of those that floats first through his mind. Unless, of course, you are NOT the right person for a start-up situation, in which case your name will not enter his thoughts … which is PERFECT, because that is not your strength. See how this can work?

But this is not where you are – you do not have a brand (I am assuming) that is well known and well understood … maybe even not to you. You will not get phone calls right or wrong with opportunities. Let's change that. Again, this starts with your own personal identification of core, valuable strengths.

WIIFM? IE, WHAT'S IN IT FOR ME?

Let's pause on this for a second, because we also need to look at this problem from the opposite direction – the hiring manager. If I'm one of these potential hiring managers looking at you for a job, don't expect me to immediately recognize your genius. We've established that you're a different breed of cat, to say the least. And your whole story line, if you really think about it, is RISK – you are going to take chances and push the organization in a new way. So, whose phone is eventually going to start ringing? Not yours, but mine as your boss!

There are going to be a number of people who will present themselves as risk takers for every one who's actually good at it. That's hard for me, as the hiring manager, to differentiate. I also may or may not be any good at identifying those characteristics that set apart high-potential change agents and innovators from those who simply aspire to it. Don't assume I can just 'tell'.

The hiring process that I'm going through is one that, eventually, reflects back on me. I need something done. I want it to be successful. I want to grow my career as a leader, and my hiring reflects that. I want to drive something new, and I fundamentally understand this involves risk, but there's a big difference between that fundamental understanding and the courage to make that call. It's much, much easier for me to go a safer route and hire a familiar, experienced candidate.

So, how are you going to convince me to change that mind-set? The answer – you are not! Instead, your job is to convince me you *are* the smart bet, the person who reduces my overall risk because of how you approach the work, rather than heightening it.

A big part of this is being honest with who you are, not just with yourself but with that hiring manager. In doing so, you may find that you actually eliminate yourself from some jobs, either because who you are is a bad fit for that role OR a bad fit for that organization & manager. Of course, this is good! The sooner this can happen, really, the better. It would be ideal if the recruiter, right on the phone, would eliminate you in those situations, saving everybody quite a bit of time.

TAKING OWNERSHIP OF YOU, INC.

You are the 100% shareholder in You, Inc. You make the decisions. You are the most precious stock You will ever own. You, Inc. will contribute more to your retirement than any other investment. And, yet, I run into people all the time who are very talented but not getting promoted. They're frustrated, they're talented, they're yearning for that next developmental step. For reasons that are often understandable, they're not getting those opportunities inside their current companies. They're often asked by their employers to "just wait", "trust the process", "your turn will come" … or, my favorite, "You need more time in-role / at-level / more laterals".

This could all be true! But, practically, isn't that up to you? You know that, right? Unless you are one of the very few who have a contract, you *can* just leave tomorrow. You are capable of building a network, cultivating career opportunities, and occasionally taking one.

Not believing this is effectively handing over 'A' level stock in You, Inc. to your employer or your boss. Shame on you! You've given up your voting rights! Never, ever do this. You own You, Inc. Make your own decisions. Never leave You, Inc. in the hands of somebody else, somebody whom for no fault of their own may someday just have to let you go as soon as right now.

I'm not telling you to leave your current company. I'm just reminding you that YOU are in charge of that decision. If you're stuck, or frustrated, or stunted … is that about *them* or *you*?

But how does You, Inc. (ie, You) make such hard decisions?

I'll start by sharing a story of when I bought Apple stock back in the summer of 2013. During this particular stretch, the investment community was getting pretty chippy with Apple and complaining of a lack of innovation. They were reacting to rumors about the next iPhone model that didn't sound particularly compelling, and the stock took a big dip, cut almost in half from its all-time highs. I bought a *ton* of Apple stock. Then, after the release of the new iPhone model and the (unsurprisingly) stellar sales, the stock took a huge gain. I made a killing on that stock.

Because I consider myself fairly sharp when it comes to managing my portfolio, I remember walking along one day and thinking about whether it was time to sell on Apple. I reminded myself that it wasn't about the returns I *had* gotten from the stock, which made me happy and very affectionate toward that holding ... it was about whether It bought I could achieve similarly outsize returns going forward, or if that money would be better put to use in another holding.

Suddenly, I had a lightbulb moment. That same thinking needed to be put into Brian Pittenger, Inc. Not to be immodest, but if a person had bought shares of Brian Pittenger, Inc. back in the early 2000's, they would have been delighted about the returns they would have seen by 2013. Heck, even shareholder who'd gotten in during 2010 would have seen really strong returns. But, at that point of my career and in the company I worked for, I realized that the path ahead may not have the same upward trajectory. At that company, my growth may have *at least* started to slow down.

I had worked for that company more than 15 years, and during that time I had been treated very, very well. I had friends, invested colleagues and management that had shepherded me along. I owed them a lot. But, of course, most of the critical stakeholders in Me, Inc. had very strong interests in managing my costs carefully. Rampant promotions, bonuses or otherwise were not in the best interests of Them, LLC.

The only person who *truly* wanted me to surge forward in title, opportunities and compensation was Me!

But, still ... this isn't an easy decision. So here's another thing to think about. If you have spent enough time with one company, they know an awful lot about you. They've seen you succeed, but they've also seen your screw-ups. They saw you flub that presentation. They saw you over-spend on that project. They remember the time that you whined when you didn't get a promotion, or when you lost your temper over a decision you didn't agree with.

In other words, if you spend enough time with one company, you've essentially moved into your mom's basement. Yes, you're a big boy now and you know so very much, but she also remembers when you wet the bed, she knows you get fussy when you don't eat lunch by 11:30 and that you prefer that the French fries DO NOT TOUCH the other food on your plate. It's awfully hard to look at a person as CEO material when you have that kind of information about somebody, even when they're *your* kid.

Additionally, if you've lived long enough in Mom's basement, you might start to believe some of that feedback. If somebody knows all your flaws, they can bring them up in every performance review and they can *always* rationalize why you're not getting promoted this year. It's easy! "Keep working on your presentation style," they can just pull out of a hat. And if you're loyal enough, you might just start to agree with them – "I need to improve my presentation style, and *then* I'll be a Director," you'll say to yourself.

Sigh.

Are you a flawed person? You sure are. Especially you, maybe. But so are They, and it didn't stop Them from getting to management, and it doesn't have to stop you.

Remember, what is the most important part of getting the job you want? Is it great hair? All the right "experiences"? A tremendous interview? NO! The most important part of getting the job you want is for SOMEBODY TO WANT TO GIVE YOU THAT JOB. Period.

Are you *doing* that?

MAKING WHAT YOU'RE WORTH

If you're successful at being at innovator – if – then you have a little something I like to call 'leverage'. And you can use that leverage to negotiate your salary to make sure you're being paid what you deserve.

If you're successful at being an innovator – if – you should be paid more than average because you are, by nature, taking higher risks than others. You have a higher likelihood of having a string of time where you do not get paid at all. Or, said differently, you can get your butt fired.

Before I go much farther, I want to stress the repeated use of 'if' in the previous paragraph. It's a big 'if'. Concerns that immediately spring to my mind related to this guess-work on your behalf:

1) You're wrong – you have completely mis-evaluated yourself and your behaviors & results. Many, many people do this. A red flag here would be if *you* happen to be your own biggest fan.

2) You're right, but they don't know it – in this case, you are completely correct that you are an innovator of the highest caliber. Unfortunately, you have been innovating inside a silo where nobody pays any attention. In other words, you're an NFL-level quarterback who plays at a Division III school in Alaska.

3) You're right, and they know it – this is, um, the 'good one'.

So I'm going to continue on for the #3's in the group, okay. The rest of you need to do some soul searching.

Anyhoo, if you're a #3, you should be getting paid. And you can negotiate that, although 99% of you will simply not do so. You don't like confrontation, you worry about what could go wrong, and you certainly don't know what you're doing. Hell, what are you even worth? I mean, what are you *asking* to get? What's fair?

You don't know, right?

That's okay. You are *supposed* to be bad at negotiating your salary. There will (probably) only be 3 or 4 times in your career that you'll really get a chance to do so. If you go to the gym 3 or 4 times in your life, with five to ten years between those sessions, you will neither enter nor win any strongman competitions.

So you'll suck at this. That's okay! Lean into it. Flip the conversation around – this is not a date. You are not hoping to get a 'second chance' to look better than your first impression. You can be bad at it – you can seem as awkward and non-poised and uneducated as you want – as long as you *get* what you want. The journey makes literally no difference in this case – just the destination & outcome.

The people on the other side of the negotiation will be better at it than you, and this horrifies all of you. You hate appearing stupid. I get it! In fact, let me play out a very poorly orchestrated version of events for you in the scripted scenario below. Some of you will laugh at this sequence of events, but I bet that when *you* play this conversation out in your heads, it doesn't go much different.

> YOU: *[Entering boss's office] I would like a raise?*
>
> BOSS/HR: *[No response, not even looking up from their desk]*
>
> YOU: *Um ... hello? Raise, please?*

*BOSS/HR: [Loud sigh]. What on *earth* makes you think you should get more money?*

YOU: I am do good. So much. [You hold your hands wide apart for emphasis] So much.

BOSS/HR: [Grabs any random sheet of paper]. It says here that people who do your job only make $4.00 an hour.

YOU: That's not even minimum wage!

BOSS/HR: [Shrugs]. That's what our data says. We paid $1.2 million to get this info. What do you have?

YOU: I did a Google.

*BOSS/HR: [Looking increasingly concerned]. In fact, looking at this sheet of paper now, I think we need to *cut* your pay by 40%.*

YOU: No! But, but ... I am do good!

*BOSS/HR: Frankly, even the fact that you would dare step into this office and ask for such an insidious thing as *money* really grinds my gears. You have some nerve.*

YOU: I just wanted ...

BOSS: [Clicks 3 random keys on keyboard]. And look at this! Your last review says that you once led a meeting that could have been better! So, you're not even that good at your job at all!

YOU: But the company made $100 zillion with my ...

*BOSS/HR: I will never, *ever* look at you the same way, or respect you, and every future promotion you ever might have had is now cancelled. [Presses new button on keyboard]*

[ADMIN ENTERS ROOM]. What's going on?

BOSS/HR: This person is just working here for the money!

[ADMIN LOOKS AT YOU WITH SAME EXPRESSION YOU WOULD USE WHEN LOOKING INTO ANOTHER PERSON'S TOILET BOWL BEFORE THEY FLUSHED].

ADMIN: My god ...

BOSS/HR: [Looking back at you]. How many children do you have?

YOU: Wait, what? Children ... what difference ...?

BOSS/HR: Just answer the question! I didn't start this conversation – *you* did with your insane focus on money! Now – how many kids do you have and where are they *right now*?

YOU: [Sobbing]. TWO! I have two children and they're at pre-school!

Yeah, not so good. Again, they've done this before and they are going to be more ready for the conversation than you. They'll make you feel bad for asking. Accept it.

The number one thing that bothers people and throws off the conversation is 'awkward pauses', which you will have plenty of because you will need to stop to think. You need to get comfortable with awkward pauses.

You can bet that HR will say things to you along the lines of: "We have never paid above this level before," or, "You are already at the 97th percentile of your salary range." These sound like compelling points, unless of course you actually stop to think about them.

For example, I once had an employee who was recruited by the Training organization to move back to their team. They offered him no increase in title and only 2% more in base salary. He was obviously flustered by this. I told him to negotiate. When he did, the HR team came back to him and said, "If we give you more, you'll be the highest paid person at your pay grade in the company!" He felt bad about this, I guess, but when he came back to me and told me what they'd said, I reminded him that, statistically, *somebody* had to be the highest paid person in his pay grade. I asked him, Did he have other people in mind at his pay grade that he wanted to be sure his compensation would stay below? I reminded him that the Training team had came to him, not the other way around.

The very next offer from HR ended up getting him a 20% increase. In exchange for almost $15,000 more per year for as long he chose to work with the company, he had to have a couple awkward exchanges with HR. It was probably a total of, like, 6 minutes of conversation.

You are not trying to win the conversation. You are trying to make more money. But you've got to play.

WHY ALL OF THIS STILL PROBABLY WON'T WORK

Hiring managers rely on their HR people. HR people rely on two things: succession plans and requirements. In an HR person's wet dream, there is either a direct succession plan for filling a role (if Job A is open, insert Person B) or there is a corporate list of 'top talent' that has been pre-identified and can be easily sourced to fill an open role. "Look at these," the HR person will say to the hiring manager, hoping that somebody's name on that list will shut him up so they can close the requisition.

Mostly, though, those open jobs get posted and people internal-and-external apply for those jobs. The HR person gets first crack at sorting through any pile that exists, looking for obviously unqualified candidates or other triggers for elimination. Whoever makes it through that review gets to the hiring manager. At either desk, your resume alone – and here I'm talking about YOUR resume, the innovator who's been skipping between functions and pyramids throughout your career – will not make a shitload of sense. If the job opening exists because the previous Director was fired for systematically hiring all the wrong people and asking them to do all the wrong things, the role SCREAMS for not just somebody with experience … but somebody with experience doing turnarounds. But to the HR person, they're thinking 'Accountant', because that's what the job description says. So, if you're the world's single greatest turnaround expert who also happens to have done jobs in Treasury, HR, Recruiting and Operations … odds are your resume ain't getting a second look.

Unless … unless you have designed that resume just-so to support your awesome Turnaround Specialist brand. Then, and only then, might you get a pause … a small crack through which it might occur that you are just the person needed. But, still, I'd give your odds at 10-20% of even getting a call. Your odds go up significantly if somebody specifically recommended you to that hiring manager or HR person because of your specialty, but you can still get so easily buried. People are trained to get roles filled and all so often that comes down to easy, logical choices and candidates … not the risk you would impose by emphasizing your capabilities over your specific job experience & titles.

The bottom-line of all of this is that the burden is on you to craft the story of who you are and to make that story well-known (or, better still, *legend*) in your organization. You need to make it so your resume and reputation scream out what you are the *best* at, and then use your experiences to support that story. You need advocates who will reach out to HR partners and hiring managers to advocate for you … ideally using the very same 'story' we're talking about here. You need to get good at all of this. And, then, you have a chance!

Hey - it's not like I recommended you go this way!

CHAPTER NINE: A SIGNIFICANT WASTE OF YOUR VALUABLE TIME

(Or, some half-baked ideas your company could implement to nurture innovators, but ultimately won't)

In this Chapter I'm going to introduce a series of ideas that could be used by any company to try to change its culture to be one that thrives with innovation instead of rejects it. Or, maybe not. Perhaps you disagree with my ideas. I will be the first person to admit they are, at best, half-baked.

But they don't have to be the exact ideas you might implement. There may be nothing more than a sentence or a kernel of a thought that I introduce in these pages where you say: "Hey, I could do something with *that*."

But why do companies *want* innovators? None of the ideas in the rest of this chapter are going to implemented if a Culture of Innovation is not desired?

Ultimately, I lean back on the idea that, especially in this day-and-age, the pace of evolution in all industries is off the charts. What will Retail look like by 2030? Or, employment in general? Will talent come to companies only from local markets, or will we all truly be world-wide freelancers? What will higher education look like in the next 10-20 years given the projections of cost increases that well exceed the potential growth in salaries? Will more kids go the direct route and get 'trade-like' apprenticeships? Will companies continue to spend tens (or hundreds) of millions building national HQ locations for their companies now that people have more technology at their homes than they have in the workplace?

And on, and on. These are problems that need ideation and new approaches to absorb and solve. These are problems that will require evolution in leadership. Or, said differently, innovation.

So, on to my crappy ideas. Enjoy!

IDEA: LEADER TENURE SHOULD BE CONTROLLED

In pro sports there is a phenomenon known as having a 'contract year'. It derives from the fact that player contracts are limited – they have a clear date when the relationship with the team (and the compensation associated) will end. At the end of that tenure, both sides may mutually agree to write a new deal with a new timeline involved and with new compensation, but that new deal, too, will have a point where it ends.

What this does is to remind both sides that compensation is tied to performance, and that performance should benefit both sides. It means that players will continue to work to maintain or even improve their performance. It means that as the definition of 'excellence' involves, so too must the performance of the player.

Teams, therefore, have an incentive to continuously evaluate and define performance, because they must use that definition (and their evaluations) to determine who to pay, and how much. They need to understand their bench and farm system, and they're incentivized to invest in both to find potential stars of tomorrow.

Players understand that a drop-off in performance, or a failure to understand that what matters now is 3-point shooting instead of pure height, will cost them. They will seek out what gets paid the most and try to not only improve those skills but will try to prove that they have them.

The concept of a 'contract year' – where both the player and team know that there is a looming decision to write a new contract based on present performance – does not exist in the business world. There is no point in which an organization's and employee's incentives are so perfectly aligned.

Maybe it should? Of course, I remind you that these ideas are, at best, half-baked. Nobody will ever actually implement this. But maybe there's some version of it that would work?

IDEA: CROWD-SOURCE YOUR INCENTIVES

Here is a non-profound thought: Incentive programs at large companies are tricky. It's hard to design a program that will create all the correct motivations without creating some incentives that are actually *against* the company's best interests. That's why bonus programs at large companies are continuously changing, in an attempt to re-direct and re-focus all incentives toward the most optimal goals.

One aspect of this challenge is this: What happens when I *exceed* the goals of the company? How much should I share in the 'upside' I deliver above the goals you set for me? Let's say I'm the lead salesperson or merchant for the typewriter division. Now, typewriter sales are not setting the world on fire these days, but there's still a surprisingly large market and a decent profit to be made. The few remaining companies in the typewriter space are fighting for market share. So, I have been tasked to grow typewriter sales in my division by 3% in the coming year. And, theoretically, I'm out designing a program that can get me that 3%.

What I am probably *not* doing is designing a program that *could* get me 15% growth. Or, at least, I've never been part or partner to a team that approached the planning / target-setting process this way. If 3% gets me the bonus I want, I'm going to deploy my resources to ensure that 3% rather than take on the challenges (across my finances, resources or time) to pursue a much larger goal that *could* be possible. Remember, as your lead sales-person or merchant, I'm the one who knows best if this is even possible.

Plus, my bonus tops out at 150% of 'target', so while I certainly will get a return on achieving more than the desired 3% growth, I definitely do not share in the growth that would get me to 15%. If anything, that 15% growth would only make my challenge even more difficult next year! So, even with the incentive programs you've put in place, my incentives as your sales leader are certainly not aligned with yours as owner.

We have a classic information asymmetry problem – I know much more about what's possible and how much work it would take to achieve than you do as the owner. People have been attempting to design around this problem for years when it comes to building bonus plans, to some avail … but certainly not as well as owners would like.

So, to that extent, here's an idea (half-baked) presented with the ideal of turning that on its head. I'm sure with some time you can make this idea better for your industry / business / culture, but here are the bare bones of it: Create a program where the sales person indirectly reveals to you their information as part of setting their own incentives.

How does it work?

1) Design (at least) 2 different incentive programs for your head of sales / merchandising / operations. One is a Conservative plan that provides relative guarantees for overall bonus payouts if certain low-end targets are achieved. In the example above, perhaps you'd say the bonus target for growth in typewriter sales would be 1% in the coming year, with an ability to grow that bonus further if you can get sales growth as high as 3%.
The other incentive Plan is an Aggressive model which pays much, much more for achieving typewriter sales growth rates closer to 10% and accelerates all the way out to 15%. The trick to the Aggressive Plan is that it pays *less* for growth at 3% than the Conservative Plan, but (as I said) much, much more if higher growth is achieved & possible.

CHART 9.1

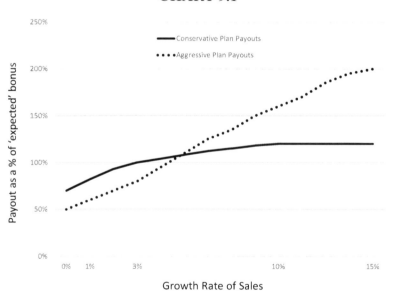

2) Offer your head of Sales (or Merch or Ops) these two options. Allow them to decide how they and their team will be incentivized in the coming year – either the Conservative or Aggressive Plan.

3) After all leaders have chosen their plans for the coming year, collect the results and study it as management. Information will emerge! If *everybody* chooses the Conservative plan, this is a signal to you that confidence is low on typewriter sales in the coming year. Explore this! Something in your product line, sales plan or competition is making everybody search for financial guarantees in their pay versus 'chasing the upside'. You, as leaders, have work to do to overcome this! Conversely, if everybody is choosing the Aggressive plan, you have an equally interesting exploration to do. Theoretically your sales team sees upside beyond what you did as owner and incentive plan designer. This might be a tremendous time to invest in additional sales people, new products … or perhaps just reach out to the competition and consider buying them out! Finally, if you have a 'mix' of people choosing Aggressive versus Conservative plans, this, too, can be telling. Perhaps certain sales teams are simply lower performers than others. Talk to them – find out why they see less upside than their peers! Perhaps upgrades are needed in your staff, or new investments in their specific markets to provide them the same opportunities for growth as their peers.

These opportunities would be *lost* if you did not have a way of comparing them before the year started … all of which is possible by surveying your team via their choice of incentive plans.

IDEA: TEACH LEADERS HOW TO SPOT INNOVATORS (AND WHAT COMES NEXT)

Many, if not most, companies have some process that the executive team goes through to identify up-and-coming talent. If you've ever been part of that conversation, you'll know that most leaders are not very good at it.

I'm not going to criticize executives for selecting some people as 'future leaders' only to discover that those people ended up becoming busts. There's a lot more people who fail than succeed at reaching that level, and the key aspects that ultimately differentiate the people who make it from those who don't can't always be identified, even after-the-fact. How people respond to extreme stress, their resilience level and thickness of skin, their ability to select good risks from bad ones, their ability to hire the best talent and more can ultimately sink an executive who, until that point, had looked like a sure-fire future CEO. Even bad timing and bad luck can undermine performance.

No, what I'm talking about here is that most executives who are faced with selecting their heir apparent and/or otherwise identifying the future leaders of the organization are simply not good at it. They often end up identifying people who remind them of themselves, or people they've come to rely upon for their deep knowledge of the systems and operations that keep the ship moving each and every day. They feel appreciative of these people, and things rarely go wrong with them in charge. They feel the company owes it to them to give them a chance to continue moving up. And, it simply does not.

What the next generation of leadership requires is *not* the same as what the previous generation required. Literally everything has changed over the years. So if that leadership group is being picked out in any way due to their resemblance to current leadership, you're in trouble.

So, if leaders are this bad at finding and selecting the *best* talent in their organization, how can they be any good at finding innovators? After all, these people may not even be on their day-to-day radar screen the way 'top talent' should be. Which is in itself the answer we're looking for in this situation – how do you *get* these kind of performers onto leaders' radar?

The answer is that it should be happening in very much the same process that companies are identifying their top talent. On a quarterly basis, leaders and their management teams should be sitting down for talent conversations. In those conversations, the standard questions should be discussed:

1) Who can we not afford to lose? Why? What can we do to appreciate these people, *and* what would be necessary to mitigate our dependence on them?

2) Who is going to replace the top leadership in our [team / pyramid / c-suite]? We should identify at least 2 people at every level that we're monitoring – Director, Manager, non-Manager.

3) For our top talent that we just identified, what risks are we asking them to take on our behalf? What have they been forced to do that stretches their comfort level and tests their readiness for higher-level roles? Who are their mentors?

4) Who are our flight risks? What would be necessary to reduce those risks? Are we willing to perform those mitigation steps? Why or why not?

But, the questions that don't often make it into that talent conversation would sound like this:

5) Who out in our teams is finding new ways to get work done? Who has surprised us with results that specifically was not done the way we would have expected?

6) Who failed at what we asked them to do? I'm not talking about day-to-day tasks that need to be performed – that would be the sign of a problem performer. I'm talking about somebody who took on a challenge and did not succeed, whether that was turning around a failing manufacturing plant, improving our intern program, or whatever.

7) If we can answer #6 above with a clear set of people, let's ask ourselves: What went wrong? What did they learn? Did they grow from the experience? Since we know this group is willing to take on risks, what new challenges do we want to assign to them? We need to find out if they *can* be successful innovators, or if it's just possible they don't have what it takes. Only through providing multiple chances can we find out.

8) If we answer #6 above without a clear group of people – are we challenging our talent enough? Are we providing opportunities for people to lead?

IDEA: FLUID HEADCOUNT REALLOCATION

Again, there is zero chance your company will implement this. But, for the sake of completion, I present it here. So let me start by saying: Wouldn't it be nice if you could say this about your company:

1) We are able to tackle new strategic projects without growing the organization's headcount

2) We continuously and aggressively eliminate the least-valuable work we're asking from our team

3) We know exactly where our best ideas come from, positioning those people to become our leaders of the future.

Sound interesting? Sure it does! You won't do it, but it's neat, huh?

For the purposes of beating this dead horse, let me continue. I worked 25 years in corporate America with almost 15 of that as a leader of teams. I also worked many of those years in Finance. So, I have both led many an annual budgeting process *and* been subjected to them. One commonality of every budget process I've been part of – every single one, every single year – is that when it came time to build my team's budget, I could pretty much count on the fact that my headcount for the next fiscal year is going to be set at the exact same number as what it was the last fiscal year. Oh, on occasion the number would have gone up-or-down based on layoffs or strategic investments involving my team, but those things tended to happen *outside* of the annual budget process. The budget itself was pretty rote about headcount, and was pretty much designed to prevent more headcount from being created, not for reducing it.

And, I understand why this is – headcount is not considered very fluid. The reasons for that are obvious. But in an attempt to be simultaneously upsetting and confusing, I present this question: Does it have to be that way?

What if the annual budgeting process was integrated more seamlessly into the annual strategic process for the organization? In this, every manager would be involved with leadership in creating and setting strategic expectations that were aligned to their headcount.

Let me present an example. Let's say I am a finance manager at ACME, Inc. I have a team of 10 analysts reporting to me. Each year I would start knowing that, at the end of the year, I was expected to return 2 of those headcount back to the company 'pool' for purposes of re-allocating toward the organization's most strategic efforts. Therefore, my goals for the current year MUST include some efforts I will undertake to make my team's work more efficient, because I must start the year with the understanding that my headcount will be reduced by 2 at year's-end.

I can achieve those efficiencies technologically or through remediation (ie, cutting work that is less important than other work). In approaching my team's work this way, it assures the company of a few things: 1) as a leader, I am always working to reduce costs, 2) we're a company that naturally attacks and eliminates its least effective work (and how many companies can actually say that?!?), and 3) I am incentivized to continuously evolve, which is healthy for me as a leader, my team and the company. I cannot simply keep running things as they've always been run!

In the same example, when the annual strategy-and-budget process does come along, the real fun begins. As a leader in that organization, I will now participate in a process where I submit my own strategic ideas for our next fiscal year into the 'bucket' alongside those of my peers and leadership. Those ideas will be vetted by executive leadership based on value, merit and alignment with the organization's executive goals. Those ideas that are the best will get funded with headcount, and that headcount will no longer be incremental to the organization since it will come from the 'pool' we created. Therefore, if my ideas as a Finance leader are strong, I will be rewarded with new headcount that may actually grow my team back to 10 (or higher), though with an explicit demand to utilize that headcount to deliver on the strategies I sold to leadership.

The company's costs do not go up, its flexibility remains continuously at peak levels, accountability is through the roof and it truly sends a message to the company that executives are 'walking the talk' by allocating significant resources according toward its declared strategies.

In addition, you will begin to figure out and differentiate who your truly strategic leaders are. You will truly start to see which people 'keep the lights on' versus who understands how to utilize your company's assets to produce new and exciting results. This kind of information is extraordinarily useful for management as it develops its leaders and finds the C-suite of tomorrow.

There are a few things to remember about this (potential) process:

1) As managers are tasked to deliver 20% of their headcount back to the organization each year, care should be taken that they do not deliver problem performers into that pool. The 'pool of resources' that you're creating should be your best talent, not your worst. HR is important to this as their

knowledge of each team and the performance management processes they lead will become an important check to prevent abuse.

2) As strategic ideas are submitted by leaders, they must be asked if resources are necessary from any partner teams. For example, as a Finance Manager if my idea involves IT or HR support, I must submit resourcing requests for those teams as well.

3) Accountability is key – if I promise that my idea will deliver $1 million in new profits to the organization, I must also declare (up front) *how* I will be measuring this result. There should be (at least) quarterly check-ins on progress. Get the $1 million!

4) If you are going to expect a 20% efficiency and remediation improvement from teams each year (to fund your headcount reallocation process), you need to do your part by hiring the leadership talent that can get you there. There is efficiency everywhere, but seizing it is not in many people's DNA. If you're not getting the efficiencies you expect each year from your leaders … some of that blame comes back to you.

5) Finally, it must occur to you that 'freeing up headcount' to reallocate to other projects/teams sounds an awful lot like layoffs. Not necessarily, and not what I intend. First of all, since we've already agreed above that you need to submit your best talent for re-assignment each year, this kind of general athlete can be useful in a lot of different ways. You're not firing these people.

Second, you need a process (especially in the second half of each year) where natural attrition is used as an opportunity to start seizing positions to 'hold' until the next year.

Finally … if after everything you start to realize you're not achieving your headcount reallocation goals and the talent remaining to choose from is not re-allocatable, you may have to consider a RIF.

Like I said at the start, this is all theoretical anyway – you're not *actually* going to implement this plan.

CHAPTER TEN: Officially, *legally*, I have to say that I'd still recommend you didn't

(Or, last words of advice)

Hey, you made it to the end of the book! Look at you!

I'm going to presume that *most* of you have arrived at this chapter as you're scouring through looking for the instructions on how to get a refund. Sorry, we pre-bent all the bindings to prevent just that.

We've covered a lot of ground in this book. It's my belief that without understanding the conditions that create resistance to innovation, you are facing an impossible task in what you're trying to do. So we spent a lot of time in the first 3 chapters trying to help you understand where that resistance comes from – the very nature of organizations, the path that leaders take, the mis-incentives that are in every organization. Without an ability to understand this and to be able to continuously diagnose your own organization, you will face increasing odds against success.

We then shifted to the work ahead, the actual act of running your initiative, idea or project through to completion. This is arduous work. Without great teams, the support of your leaders, an understanding of the problems you will face or the tools that you need, you once again are facing an uphill battle. Chapters 4 thru 7 are my attempt to arm you for that.

You're doing all of this for a reason, and Chapter 8 talks about building your career as an innovator, rather than climbing the traditional corporate ladder.

Chapter 9 is my (admittedly) feeble attempt to provide ideas that might make all of this advice obsolete, the kind of ideas that I would hope could help make companies more conducive to continuous innovation and evolution. Why would companies want this? Because without perpetual evolution, companies will eventually disappear … just like 87% of all companies have since the very first Fortune 500 list almost 100 years ago have disappeared.

And here we are. My last words of advice are against everything I've said to this point – you *can* do this. It can be lonely, and there are not college classes or career conferences you can attend that will teach you. But the tools are all here for you, and the key to everything, as always … is you.

And I wish you the very best with it. Your company *needs* you to be successful.

AFTERWORD

I take great passion in these ideas, but I know they are not all correct. They are intended to stimulate your own ideas, much as I have taken the thoughts and considerations of others and (over the course of decades) formed my own thoughts about how things can be.

Also, I love these conversations and I love that I'm nowhere close to done learning. If you want to start a conversation, or continue one, with me, you can find me at:

Website: www.moneybuttonbook.com

LinkedIn: www.linkedin.com/in/brianapittenger

E-Mail: brian.pittenger@moneybuttonbook.com

Twitter: @PittengerEvents

Thank you for enjoying this ride with me (or not). For me, this is a culmination of a dream. I hope I didn't screw it up too badly.

No refunds.

ACKNOWLEDGEMENTS

First of all, a shit-ton of the thoughts and ideas I've shared on these pages were developed over many years by practicing them on what was basically a hostage group – those people who worked for me and couldn't just get up and run away when I would start philosophizing. To them, I give my greatest apologies and thank you's.

There have been a few extremely formative people in my career, those who bring exciting ideas to the table and from whom a lot of my ideas were grown. John Mulligan, John Jantson, Elizabeth Weber, John Brockman, Jeff Miller, Thad Hellman, Valerie Conard, Kristine Boedigheimer, Dave Caspers, Scott Brill, Mike Robbins, Jay Smith, Michael Fiddelke, Mark Merrill, Mike Stigers, Mark Gross, Kelley Wedeking, Jackie Hartman, Dave Archer, Greg Kerkvleit, John Hulbert, Barb Kosloski, Dan Stavedahl, Christy Powers, Steffen Meyer, Tim Curoe, Jeff Elston, Tony Willoughby, Frank Miller, Travis Colvin, Aaron Johnson, Ben Matthews, Sean Trevis, Omar Reece, Dawne Carlson, Sara Boe, Dave Warren, Renee Oertli and so many more that I'll cringe later when I remember their names and the influences they have had on me. Thanks to all of you!

A special shout-out to Erica DeForrest, without whom I never would have even started this book. Any claims she has beyond that are outright lies. My lawyer suggests we're on good grounds for this one.

Some of my greatest influences also came from other writers' thinking. I obviously owe a lot to Nassim Nicolas Taleb, Scott Adams, Adam Corolla, Jeffrey Cohn, Jay Moran, Michael Eisner,

Seth Godin, Marshall Goldsmith, Reid Hoffman, Jeff Jarvis, Gary Keller, Chuck Klosterman, Steven Levitt, Stephen Dubner, Tom Peters, Geoff Smart, Randy Street, Michael Watkins, Dave Barry, Ann Salerno and Lillie Brock. I'm sure the list goes farther, but you will find their influence prevalent in this book.

To my parents. You know, I never know how to thank my parents enough. I mean, they must have done some really great stuff, because I feel like I've managed to lead a pretty good life, and that's got to be a huge reward for a parent. But, I was also so self-absorbed that I didn't really notice what they were doing. So, here goes: To my parents, whose humor and pragmatism must have rubbed off, and for whom I am eternally grateful.

Finally, to my wife, Pam, and my kids, Parker & Payton, who patiently put up with every strange idea I have, even when that involves quitting my job to write a book. It's the kind of idiot move that they haven't yet come up with a good argument against, and for that, I *thank you* and *love you all*.

Brian, Feb 2018

INDEX:

[i] Crichton, Michael. *Jurassic Park*. Random House Publishing Group, 1990.

[ii] Personal Interview. "Tonya". Feb 12, 2018. (Audio Recording)

[iii] Fortune Magazine, Fortune 500 from 1955.
http://archive.fortune.com/magazines/fortune/fortune500_archive/full/1955/

[iv] What Does Fortune 500 Turnover Mean? By Dane Stangler and Sam Arbesman, Ewing Marion Kauffman Foundation, June 2012.
http://www.kauffman.org/~/media/kauffman_org/research%20reports%20and%20covers/2012/06/fortune_500_turnover.pdf

[v] Personal Interview. "Cathy". Feb 20, 2018. (Audio Recording)

[vi] Photo used with permission. Licensed via iStockPhoto, 2018.

[vii] Personal Interview. "Mark". Feb 20, 2018. (Audio Recording)

[viii] Eisner, Michael. *Working Together: Why Great Partners Succeed*. Harper Collins, 2010.

[ix] Adams, Scott. *Dogbert's Management Handbook*. Harper Collins, 1996.

[x] Personal Interview. "Rich". Feb 8, 2018. (Audio Recording)

[xi] Salerno, Ann and Brock, Lillie. *The Change Cycle: How People Can Survive and Thrive in Organizational Change*. Berrett-Koehler Publishers, Inc, 2008.

[xii] *Inglourious Basterds*. Quentin Tarantino. Universal Pictures, The Weinstein Company, A Band Apart. 2009.

[xiii] Personal Interview. "Marta". Feb 18, 2018. (Audio Recording)

95713471R00113

Made in the USA
Columbia, SC
14 May 2018